Understanding Foreign Policy Commentary

Daniel Mobley • Joe Gazeley

Understanding Foreign Policy Commentary

palgrave
macmillan

Daniel Mobley
REPI
Université libre de Bruxelles
Brussels, Belgium

Joe Gazeley
University of St Andrews
St Andrews, UK

ISBN 978-3-031-95472-6   ISBN 978-3-031-95473-3   (eBook)
https://doi.org/10.1007/978-3-031-95473-3

© The Editor(s) (if applicable) and The Author(s), under exclusive license to Springer Nature
Switzerland AG 2025

This work is subject to copyright. All rights are solely and exclusively licensed by the
Publisher, whether the whole or part of the material is concerned, specifically the rights of
translation, reprinting, reuse of illustrations, recitation, broadcasting, reproduction on
microfilms or in any other physical way, and transmission or information storage and retrieval,
electronic adaptation, computer software, or by similar or dissimilar methodology now
known or hereafter developed.
The use of general descriptive names, registered names, trademarks, service marks, etc. in this
publication does not imply, even in the absence of a specific statement, that such names are
exempt from the relevant protective laws and regulations and therefore free for general use.
The publisher, the authors and the editors are safe to assume that the advice and information
in this book are believed to be true and accurate at the date of publication. Neither the
publisher nor the authors or the editors give a warranty, expressed or implied, with respect to
the material contained herein or for any errors or omissions that may have been made. The
publisher remains neutral with regard to jurisdictional claims in published maps and
institutional affiliations.

Cover illustration: Pattern © John Rawsterne/patternhead.com

This Palgrave Macmillan imprint is published by the registered company Springer Nature
Switzerland AG.
The registered company address is: Gewerbestrasse 11, 6330 Cham, Switzerland

If disposing of this product, please recycle the paper.

ACKNOWLEDGEMENTS

The authors would like to thank those participants who gave comments at the 'Memory, Narratives, and Perceptions in World Politics' panel at BISA 2023 in Glasgow where the ideas which became this manuscript were initially presented. They would also like to thank two anonymous reviewers for their comments and Dr Gazeley would like to thank the Belgian Fund for Scientific Research (F.R.S.-FNRS).

CONTENTS

1	Introduction	1
2	Wild Realism: A Methodological and Conceptual Approach	13
3	US Foreign Policy Commentary in the Obama Era (2009–2017)	31
4	US Foreign Policy Commentary in the Trump Era (2017–2021)	47
5	US Foreign Policy Commentary in the Biden Era (2021–2024)	61
6	Conclusion	81

Postscript	87
Index	89

ABOUT THE AUTHORS

Daniel Mobley is an associate lecturer in the School of International Relations at the University of St Andrews. His research focuses on (historical) US foreign policy, critical security studies, International Relations theory, and the concept of US isolationism. He is especially interested in the constitutive functions of security discourses.

Joe Gazeley is an F.R.S.-FNRS postdoctoral research fellow at the Université libre de Bruxelles. He is an interdisciplinary researcher situated between International Relations and History. His research focuses on foreign policy, both as a practice within the postcolonial relationship between Africa and France, and as a field, as debated and understood by academics, policymakers, and the public.

List of Figures

Fig. 3.1 Graphic from an article in the March/April 2012 edition of FP by Rove and Gillespie (2012: 22) titled *How to Beat Obama*   36

Fig. 5.1 Photo montage of selected FA covers from 2021–2024. (Cover photos from: Foreign Affairs Archives | Press Reader)   63

CHAPTER 1

Introduction

Abstract This chapter introduces the concept of the Foreign Policy Commentariat (FPC) and explains the significance of the foreign policy commentary articulated in the pages of *Foreign Policy* and *Foreign Affairs* magazines. This commentary is presented as being distinct from academic analyses due to the editorial practices of these magazines and their general public audiences. The chapter also briefly outlines the chapters to follow: (2) the methodological and conceptual approach, and analyses of the (3) Obama, (4) Trump, and (5) Biden administrations.

Keywords Foreign policy commentary • International Relations • Academic writing • Audiences • Foreign Policy Commentariat

This research began with a train journey. One of the authors, catching sight of the newsagent's racks at the train station, was struck by the prominent presence of *Foreign Policy* (FP) and *Foreign Affairs* (FA) magazines. It struck this author, that given the small numbers of people who read academic International Relations (IR) journals, the survival of these titles in an era of declining print-readership posed something of a puzzle. What are these magazines which seem to exist between the specialist realm of academic IR and the mainstream world of newspapers? Who are they for? Perhaps most importantly, given that they are the most widely available and

© The Author(s), under exclusive license to Springer Nature
Switzerland AG 2025
D. Mobley, J. Gazeley, *Understanding Foreign Policy Commentary*,
https://doi.org/10.1007/978-3-031-95473-3_1

1

prestigious mainstream publications on foreign policy, how do they present this very specialist field to the general audience? This is the question which one author put to the other, and with which this Pivot seeks to engage.[1]

Both FA and FP have attracted contributors from different political traditions, professional backgrounds and with different ideas on policy. These publications have demonstrated a sustained ability to attract significant figures from the worlds of policy, academia and journalism to offer commentary on foreign policy events. They have an unparalleled reach within their niche and are the most accessible form of specialist foreign policy commentary to the general public.[2] By analysing past issues of these two publications from January 2008 to September 2024 we have sought to understand the overall vision of foreign policy which has been presented to this presumed mainstream audience by these authors as a group. We first introduce the key concept of the Foreign Policy Commentariat (FPC) to help us understand the group who publish in these outlets. In the following chapter we then present our theoretical and methodological approach. This is followed by three empirical chapters which explore how these magazines presented US foreign policy during the presidencies of Obama, Trump and Biden. We have structured our empirical analysis through the rhythms of these publications themselves, which appear to be based on the US Presidential election timetable, and each empirical chapter is demarcated by a transfer of power. The US foreign policy focus was determined by these magazines themselves, in which the most prominent, and mainstream articles were primarily concerned with US foreign policy, and which, despite their international audience, treat US foreign policy as coterminous with foreign policy in general.

We must emphasize that this book is not an attempt to disparage these publications or the authors who have contributed to them. We have the utmost respect for those who have devoted their time to disseminating knowledge through accessible media. Nor are we seeking to flatten the nuances of publications which are not monolithic—evolving even over the period of study (2008–2024)—nor to discount the value of their contributions to informing public debate of foreign policy. From our analysis we do have concerns about the relatively narrow theoretical parameters of

---

[1] This Pivot resulted from a seminar discussion at the British International Studies Association Conference 2023 in Glasgow. The authors are indebted to participants for their insightful questions and comments.

[2] Major newspapers have foreign affairs commentary but this is often less detailed, more responsive to immediate developments and shorter than a full article in FA or FP.

debate, and the editorial guidelines which shape them. Yet, these publications remain, in our view, a net-positive for public awareness of foreign policy issues by virtue of their reach, prestige, the eminent individuals they are able to attract, and their vibrant letters pages.[3]

There is a growing body of research on the relationship between the public and foreign policy, which appears to demonstrate the ignorance of the public on these matters (Council on Foreign Relations 2024; Kertzer and Zeitzoff 2017; Foyle and Van Belle 2010). Recent work has explored the role of foreign policy intellectuals on shaping policy (MacKay 2024; King 2023). Outside, or perhaps adjacent to, the ivory tower sit the think tanks, who have received their share of academic interest (Arin 2014; Higgott and Stone 1994; Medvetz 2014; Stone 1996; Niblett 2018; Ricci 1994). There remains however, very little research on the foreign policy commentary which should serve both to stimulate and inform public debate on foreign policy questions.[4] Whilst affairs of state may seem distant from the daily affairs of average citizens, they shape the ability of those citizens to live their lives in peace and prosperity. History is replete with innumerable foreign policy disasters which have caused death, misery and destruction on a scale unimaginable in almost any other field of human activity. Given the stakes of failure, the need for public scrutiny of foreign policy is clear. Foreign policy has the potential to impact all citizens yet the capacity to evaluate foreign policy depends on access to informed, specialist analysis. Providing this analysis is particularly important in democratic societies where citizens are regularly asked to consider overall governmental performance at elections, including foreign policy conduct.

Given the high paywalls erected around academic papers, and the dense and alienating language in which many of these papers are written, the public need for foreign policy knowledge is not being met by academic journals. Despite the efforts made by individual scholars to reach out and disseminate their knowledge to a general audience, this work of public commentary faces structural hurdles within academic IR. It is not greatly valued by hiring committees, tenure committees or promotions boards, certainly less than peer-reviewed publications and grants, and therefore can represent a significant opportunity cost to any but the most senior, and securely employed, academics.

---

[3] FP has dropped this which is a real shame, but FA continues the tradition of providing this genuine site for debate on articles which have been published.

[4] For research on a similar group of foreign policy commentators in a Chinese context see: Abb (2021), Hamrin and Cheek (2023) and Hao (2003).

WHAT IS FOREIGN POLICY COMMENTARY?

At its most basic foreign policy commentary is simply the act of 'commentating' on unfolding or recent foreign policy events, evaluating and situating them within a wider context. This does not require a particular partisan or policy agenda, and can range from critique to hagiography. There is no need for this commentary to be public facing, or even written down. However, there does need to be some audience, for if one engages in solo commentary then one is really just talking to oneself about the news. Commentary, in that sense is a social activity at the point of consumption, where the product of the expertise of the commentator is presumed to be consumed by an audience of some kind.

Whilst anyone can engage in foreign policy commentary as an activity, access to the top tier of public facing commentary, as represented by the journals FA and FP, is the preserve of a select few. They include serving government officials, sometimes trying to promote a policy, sometimes trying to promote themselves. For example, then Secretary of State Hillary Clinton's piece in *Foreign Policy* in 2011 was presumably calculated to display her foreign policy credentials in advance of a potential Presidential run (Clinton 2011). They could include former senior Presidential advisers such as Zbigniew Brzezinski and Karl Rove. There are also the former officials, who draw on their years of experience to give insight into 'the way things work'. These former officials overlap with the next group: the Think Tank crowd, for whom public facing commentary on foreign policy, often from a partisan position, is an expectation of their employment. Career academics also engage in foreign policy commentary, even at this rarefied level. Both FP and FA have published articles from senior academics trying to communicate new research findings, for example Keren Yarhi-Milo's piece on credibility in US foreign policy (Yarhi-Milo 2024), and from what might be termed celebrity academics such as Stephen Walt and Niall Ferguson (who have both published in FA and FP).

As individuals, the members of the FPC are difficult to pin down as they are professionally mobile, often moving across vocational boundaries. As a group, they are former and/or future policymakers and/or academics and/or journalists. To pick examples who have published in both FP and FA, Walter Russell Mead and Matthew Kroenig have moved between the think tank, journalistic and academic worlds and between the policy, academic and think tank worlds, respectively. For such figures, access to the most prestigious outlets for foreign policy commentary in the anglophone world represents the opportunity for career advancement by demonstrating the prominence of the individual in public facing foreign policy debates.

The FPC as a group could be conceptualised as Establishment Intellectuals, building on Hamrin and Cheek, who identified a group of Establishment Intellectuals in China during the 1950s–1980s that:

> ...played a key mediating role in coordinating a symbiotic exchange of services—an implicit social contract—between rulers and the larger intellectual elite. In this exchange, the intellectuals provided expertise and buttressed the moral legitimacy of the governing group by explaining and popularizing its policies. The leadership in turn gave the intellectuals the opportunity to serve the country and engage in their professional pursuits, while enjoying a relatively affluent and culturally rich lifestyle. (Hamrin and Cheek 2023: 4)

Though this definition does not fit all contributors to FP and FA over our period of study, it does help us to explain the relatively narrow bounds of debate, which we argue are self-reinforcing. In order to fit within this elite, it is necessary to frame commentary within the bounds which that elite recognises, in order to perform expertise. Now, it is necessary to highlight that Hamrin and Cheek were describing a dramatically different political system, underpinned by a different political consensus. The ties between the state and the commentator in the US vary more significantly than those of the Establishment Intellectuals that they describe from mid-twentieth century China, who were ultimately state employees, even if one step removed. This is the case for some commentators but by no means the majority, who are defined by their fluidity and the apparent ease by which they move between the state and the private sectors. Indeed, Hamrin and Cheek themselves highlight the specifically Chinese nature of the relationship they describe between elites and the state, arguing that:

> While this type of intellectual might be found in any culture, there is a particularly powerful tradition in China...whereby scholar-officials have gained tremendous political power and social stature by serving at the higher levels of state administration and as personal counselors or agents of the sovereign. In our view, this is a special stratum of intellectuals that exists only in a system in which political control of culture is widely perceived as legitimate. (Hamrin and Cheek 2023: 4)

On the specific issue of foreign policy, the relationship between the FPC and the state appears similar. The interweaving of state functions and private commentary appears a logical consequence of the dominance of the state over foreign policy. Commentary is given weight by perceived expertise, and this expertise is perhaps most concretely demonstrated through some period of government service. Commentary also allows the commentator to perform expertise, acting as a means by which an aspiring policymaker can demonstrate their credentials for government service. Given a system where many positions are political appointments, the history of US foreign policy is replete with high-profile scholar-officials such as Walt Rostow, Henry Kissinger, Zbigniew Brzezinski and Susan Rice.

Despite the participation of some academics in this form of foreign policy commentary, it is important to distinguish articles in FP and FA from academic writing. These publications are not peer-reviewed and their guidelines push authors away from theory and towards empiricism. For example, FP states that its ideal article *"strikes a balance"* and *"should spark debate among specialists but also engage a general interest reader"*.[5] Highlighting that these commentary pieces are not targeting an academic audience, their submission guidelines recommend writers *"[s]teer clear of wonky, technical language"* (ibid.). These guidelines also claim that *"[w]e edit extensively at FP"* (ibid.). Likewise, FA states in its submission guidance that it *"strives to present clear thinking by knowledgeable observers on important issues, written in English that can be read with ease and pleasure by both professionals and a broad general audience"*.[6] However, in contrast to FP their guidance also implies there is little editorial oversight: *"We rely mainly on authors to ensure the accuracy of information in their pieces"* (ibid.).

There are two key distinctions between academic writing and foreign policy commentary, as reflected in FP and FA. The first is that the presumed audiences are very different. Academic writing is often laser targeted at a specific group of scholars working on a particular problem, or at students who are being taught a particular case study or theoretical approach. FA and FP target a general audience with an interest in foreign policy. This leads to the next key distinction which is linguistic. Academics, when writing for other academics who are within their own research area are effectively communicating in the codes and lexicon of a unique

---

[5] The guidelines are available in full here: https://foreignpolicy.submittable.com/submit
[6] The guidelines are available in full here: https://www.foreignaffairs.com/submissions-0

subculture, which are neither easily intelligible to outsiders nor intended to be. In contrast, publications like FP and FA must provide foreign policy commentary in a form which is comprehensible to a general audience. This pushes this form of writing to be relatively inclusive, without sacrificing the impression that the magazine is offering some depth of insight which is not available from, for example, a broadsheet newspaper. This is a difficult balancing act and perhaps explains the prevalence in both magazines of big names (Walt, Brzezinski, Biden etc.) who can communicate in simple terms without undermining their assumed expertise in their field. Both FA and FP are more expensive than a newspaper and these big names presumably help to 'sell' these magazines as a product. Aside from the prevalence of big names inside these magazines we can also see this in their prominence on the cover. For example, it can be assumed that the FA editorial staff felt that then serving National Security Adviser Jake Sullivan was the main draw of the September 2023 issue as his name was on the front cover in large print.[7]

These publication's editorial guidelines, which favour simple terms, push texts towards an atheoretical presentation. This means that concepts which in an academic context would be presented as theoretical or conceptual tools, and therefore open to debate, redefinition or even outright rejection, are embedded in FP and FA as assumptions about the true nature of how the international system works. This suggests that academic IR and public facing foreign policy commentary are moving in two different directions. Academic writing is firmly in the realm of abstract debate in which the very conceptual framing of the key terms of that debate are themselves constantly debated. Is there such a thing as an international system? Would the nature of such a system be knowable? Even for IR scholars these debates can be exhausting to read and lead to abstract, navel-gazing theoretical explanations which call to mind Hoffman's critique of Waltzian neorealism, that "*if it is so removed* [from reality] *that what it 'explains' has little relation to what occurs, what is the use*" (Hoffmann 1977: 52)? Goh describes this tendency as academic IR's "*double divorce from real-world puzzles and from policy relevance*" (Goh 2019) and argues that:

---

[7] Two others, former US Secretary of Defense Bob Gates and Keren Yarhi-Milo, dean of the School of International and Public Affairs at Columbia University, are also honoured with space on the cover but with a smaller font.

> (1) journalists and policy analysts focused exclusively on current affairs have more impact and input into crucial areas of foreign policy—and strategy-making and debates than scholars with theoretical, historical, and area-studies expertise and (2) IR scholars with such expertise and interest in real-world policy issues have moved into public policy schools, military colleges, and policy think tanks. The latter trend facilitates disciplinary emigration and exacerbates multiple biases within the IR mainstream—over time, such scholars cease to publish in key IR journals, favoring policy- or area-studies journals instead, and the use of their scholarship to train mainstream IR accordingly declines. (ibid., p. 407)

The inverse appears to be the case for foreign policy commentary published in FP and FA. Instead of the academic slide from the concrete to the abstract, this foreign policy commentary is so focused on tangible, measurable policy debate that it does not engage with the constructed nature of the concepts that structure this world. This emphasis on policy relevant commentary on what FA's editorial guidelines term '*important issues*' has produced a public facing discourse which reflects weaknesses of an earlier period of academic IR, and another element of Hoffman's critique.[8] Hoffman was writing in the late 1970s during an era when some of the big names of IR were not confined to abstract theoretical debates—or even academia—but indeed became big names by entering government. Critiquing mainstream American IR during the era of Kissinger and Brzezinski he argued that, for the discipline:

> the key question has not been, "What should we know?" It has been, "What should we do?" about the Russians, the Chinese, the bomb, the oil producers. We have tried to know as much as we needed in order to know how to act and rarely more. (Hoffmann 1977: 59)

It is striking that, fifty years later, whilst the discipline of IR has evolved, the Foreign Policy Commentariat has taken on this role. Commentators are still concerned with what to do about Russia (King and Menon 2010; Kotkin 2024; Stonovaya 2023), China (Pottinger and Gallagher 2024; Economy 2024; Beckley 2023; Glaser et al. 2024; Harrell 2024), the bomb (Maloney 2024; Lieber and Press 2023; Kendall-Taylor and Fontaine 2024), and the oil producing Middle East (Fantappie and Nasr 2024; Robbins et al. 2024; Kaye and Vakil 2024). Whilst the academic

---

[8] The guidelines are available in full here: https://www.foreignaffairs.com/submissions-0

mainstream of IR has followed the Waltzian path towards greater abstraction, the FPC has set up shop on the terrain of public facing policy relevance, which the discipline has mostly vacated as it has become more theoretically sophisticated.

REFERENCES

Pascal Abb, 'Leaders or "Guides" of Public Opinion? The Media Role of Chinese Foreign Policy Experts', *Modern China* 47, no. 3 (1 May 2021): 320–49, https://doi.org/10.1177/0097700419882733

Kubilay Yado Arin, *Think Tanks: The Brain Trusts of US Foreign Policy* (Wiesbaden: Springer Fachmedien, 2014), https://doi.org/10.1007/978-3-658-02935-7

Michael Beckley, 'Delusions of Détente: Why America and China Will Be Enduring Rivals', *Foreign Affairs* (New York, United Kingdom: Council on Foreign Relations NY, October 2023)

Hillary Clinton, 'America's Pacific Century: The Future of Geopolitics Will Be Decided in Asia, Not in Afghanistan or Iraq, and the United States Should Be Right at the Center of the Action', *Foreign Policy*, no. 189 (2011): 56–63.

Council on Foreign Relations, 'U.S. Adults' Knowledge About the World', accessed 1 October 2024, https://www.cfr.org/report/us-adults-knowledge-about-world

Elizabeth Economy, 'China's Alternative Order: And What America Should Learn From It', *Foreign Affairs* (New York, United Kingdom: Council on Foreign Relations NY, June 2024)

Maria Fantappie and Vali Nasr, 'The War That Remade the Middle East: How Washington Can Stabilize a Transformed Region', *Foreign Affairs* (New York, United Kingdom: Council on Foreign Relations NY, February 2024)

Douglas C. Foyle and Douglas Van Belle, 'Domestic Politics and Foreign Policy Analysis: Public Opinion, Elections, Interest Groups, and the Media', in *Oxford Research Encyclopedia of International Studies*, 2010, https://doi.org/10.1093/acrefore/9780190846626.013.9

Bonnie S. Glaser, Jessica Chen Weiss, and Thomas J. Christensen, 'Taiwan and the True Sources of Deterrence: Why America Must Reassure, Not Just Threaten, China', *Foreign Affairs* (New York, United Kingdom: Council on Foreign Relations NY, February 2024)

Evelyn Goh, 'US Dominance and American Bias in International Relations Scholarship: A View from the Outside', *Journal of Global Security Studies* 4, no. 3 (1 July 2019): 406, https://doi.org/10.1093/jogss/ogz029

Carol Lee Hamrin and Timothy Cheek, *China's Establishment Intellectuals* (New York: Routledge, 2023), https://doi.org/10.4324/9781003418849

10   D. MOBLEY AND J. GAZELEY

Zhidong Hao, *Intellectuals at a Crossroads: The Changing Politics of China's Knowledge Workers* (Albany: State University of New York Press, 2003), http://archive.org/details/intellectualsatc0000haoz

Peter E. Harrell, 'How to China-Proof the Global Economy: America Needs a More Targeted Strategy', *Foreign Affairs* (New York, United Kingdom: Council on Foreign Relations NY, February 2024)

Richard Higgott and Diane Stone, 'The Limits of Influence: Foreign Policy Think Tanks in Britain and the USA', *Review of International Studies* 20, no. 1 (January 1994): 15–34, https://doi.org/10.1017/S0260210500117760

Stanley Hoffmann, 'An American Social Science: International Relations', *Daedalus* 106, no. 3 (1977).

Dalia Dassa Kaye and Sanam Vakil, 'Only the Middle East Can Fix the Middle East: The Path to a Post-American Regional Order', *Foreign Affairs* (New York, United Kingdom: Council on Foreign Relations NY, April 2024)

Andrea Kendall-Taylor and Richard Fontaine, 'The Axis of Upheaval: How America's Adversaries Are Uniting to Overturn the Global Order', *Foreign Affairs* (New York, United Kingdom: Council on Foreign Relations NY, June 2024)

Joshua D. Kertzer and Thomas Zeitzoff, 'A Bottom-Up Theory of Public Opinion about Foreign Policy', *American Journal of Political Science* 61, no. 3 (2017): 543–58, https://doi.org/10.1111/ajps.12314

Charles King, 'The Real Washington Consensus: Modernization Theory and the Delusions of American Strategy', *Foreign Affairs* (New York, United Kingdom: Council on Foreign Relations NY, December 2023).

Charles King and Rajan Menon, 'Prisoners of the Caucasus - Russia's Invisible Civil War', *Foreign Affairs* 89 (2010): 20

Stephen Kotkin, 'The Five Futures of Russia: And How America Can Prepare for Whatever Comes Next', *Foreign Affairs* (New York, United Kingdom: Council on Foreign Relations NY, June 2024)

Keir A. Lieber and Daryl G. Press, 'The Return of Nuclear Escalation: How America's Adversaries Have Hijacked Its Old Deterrence Strategy', *Foreign Affairs* (New York, United Kingdom: Council on Foreign Relations NY, December 2023)

Joseph MacKay, "Making Democracy Safe for the World": Kenneth Waltz on Realism, Democracy, and War', *International Studies Quarterly* 68, no. 3 (1 September 2024): https://doi.org/10.1093/isq/sqae112.

Suzanne Maloney, 'Iran's Order of Chaos: How the Islamic Republic Is Remaking the Middle East', *Foreign Affairs* (New York, United Kingdom: Council on Foreign Relations NY, June 2024)

Thomas Medvetz, *Think Tanks in America* (Chicago, IL: University of Chicago Press, 2014), https://press.uchicago.edu/ucp/books/book/chicago/T/bo13181062.html

Robin Niblett, 'Rediscovering a Sense of Purpose: The Challenge for Western Think-Tanks', *International Affairs* 94, no. 6 (1 November 2018): 1409–29, https://doi.org/10.1093/ia/iiy199

Matt Pottinger and Mike Gallagher, 'No Substitute for Victory: America's Competition With China Must Be Won, Not Managed', *Foreign Affairs* (New York, United Kingdom: Council on Foreign Relations NY, June 2024)

David M. Ricci, *The Transformation of American Politics: The New Washington and the Rise of Think Tanks*, Revised edition (New Haven, Conn. London: Yale University Press, 1994).

Michael Robbins, Amaney A. Jamal, and Mark Tessler, 'America Is Losing the Arab World: And China Is Reaping the Benefits', *Foreign Affairs* (New York, United Kingdom: Council on Foreign Relations NY, August 2024)

Tatiana Stanovaya, 'Putin's Age of Chaos: The Dangers of Russian Disorder', *Foreign Affairs* (New York, United Kingdom: Council on Foreign Relations NY, October 2023)

Diane Stone, *Capturing the Political Imagination: Think Tanks and the Policy Process* (London; Frank Cass, 1996).

Keren Yarhi-Milo, 'The Credibility Trap: Is Reputation Worth Fighting For?', *Foreign Affairs* (New York, United Kingdom: Council on Foreign Relations NY, August 2024).

CHAPTER 2

Wild Realism: A Methodological and Conceptual Approach

Abstract This chapter introduces the concept of Wild Realism as a means of differentiating the realism in the FPC from the theories used in academia. This concept is then situated in the book's critical methodological approach. Intersectional gender and postcolonial approaches, as well as the constructedness of analytical concepts, are explained and posited as means to problematize and understand how the Wild Realism discourse functions.

Keywords Gender • Postcoloniality • Critical approaches • Performativity • Intentionality • Positionality • Wild Realism

We wish to understand how foreign policy has been presented to a mainstream audience through *Foreign Affairs* (FA) and *Foreign Policy* (FP) magazines. In order to answer this question, we conducted a discourse analysis of selected articles from the print versions of FA and FP published between January 2008 to September 2024. Across this period FP and FA published, in total, 8410 print articles. However, not all of these articles were directly related to foreign policy. Some were letters, a large number were book reviews or special issues (for example the FP Failed States Index). Discounting such articles left a pool of 263 articles across our timeframe which were directly related to foreign policy. Of this 263, not

© The Author(s), under exclusive license to Springer Nature Switzerland AG 2025
D. Mobley, J. Gazeley, *Understanding Foreign Policy Commentary*, https://doi.org/10.1007/978-3-031-95473-3_2

13

all articles were of equal prominence so we focused on the most high-profile articles which we determined through their positioning within each issue (for example cover articles), and by the status of contributors (for example senior policymakers, celebrity academics, etc.) to try and understand the most mainstream representation of foreign policy.[1]

We have adopted the term 'Wild Realism' to describe this representation. This concept is used to interrogate the positivist approaches deployed by this august group of foreign policy commentators in their texts. The 'wild' is applied to differentiate this realism from the realisms utilised by scholars in the realm of academia. The approaches we observe in texts from this Foreign Policy Commentariat (FPC) tend to be simplified and untethered from academic foundations. The FPC rarely *uses* realism; there is no explicit application of theory to understand empirical contexts. Instead, abstracted concepts from realism—national interests, balance of power, etc.—are employed by these authors. However, they are not treated as concepts, as theoretical devices to help us understand the world. Instead, they appear to be presented as ontological, as fact.

We are not claiming that the authors in these magazines are using theories incorrectly. Instead, we argue that elements from positivist IR approaches, especially realisms, are employed in a specific discourse. We also do not claim that there is necessarily any conscious intent to articulate such a discourse. Indeed, how could there be from such a disparate group? However, we do claim such a discourse is visible in the texts of the FPC. This discourse reproduces certain understandings: about how the world of foreign policy works, how states behave, and how we should study international relations.

Our approach to understanding the FPC and conceptualizing Wild Realism is critical. Like Williams (2005), we recognize that through identifying a 'tradition' of Wild Realist discourse, we risk reifying a concept of Wild Realism and may potentially reify and legitimize "an essentially arbitrary historical claim of theoretical unity and continuity" (p. 15). Furthermore, and again following Williams (2005), we adopt Ricoeur's notion that texts are multivocal, not omnivocal (p. 15). If we think of the act of reading as a relationship—between the reader and the text—this relationship requires a respect for and an indebtedness toward the text itself, regardless of how much the reader is directed by their own interests.

---

[1] Each empirical chapter has a full list of the articles we drew on for our analysis in the 'Primary Sources' section of the bibliography.

However, there is always a distance—gaps between interpretations—so that there is no one absolute reading of a text (ibid.; see also: Crapanzano 2001). This methodological approach allows us to address the aforementioned risk of reification, as well as the potential intentions of the authors of the texts we analyse and our critical intentionality as analysts.

To help formulate our methodological approach, we turn to Michel Foucault, particularly his method of problematization. In essence, we are problematizing the discourse of Wild Realism in the texts of the Foreign Policy Commentariat. The method of problematization is a double move. The first move identifies and contextualizes the problematization, the second amplifies and further problematizes the initial intervention (Neal 2019: 43–4). This second move points to an important aspect of this method: reflexivity. We, as analysts, do not claim to hold a God's eye view from which to divine objective, ahistorical concepts—instead we have our own *positionality* and critical *intentionality*. We recognize our view is situated in a particular *position* within history, context, academic traditions, as well as identities. In addition to this, we have collected, selected, and analysed empirical data motivated by our own critical *intent* to challenge approaches and assumptions that have hitherto been un(der)challenged (ibid.).

While we identify and problematize the discourse of Wild Realism within the texts of the FPC, we neither claim that Wild Realism exists as a historical tradition with theoretical unity and continuity, nor that those who have written texts we identify as articulating a Wild Realist discourse did so intentionally as part of a theoretical tradition. Indeed, to borrow Foucault's (1980) words, within Wild Realism discourses "the logic is perfectly clear, the aims decipherable, and yet it is often the case that no one is there to have invented them, and few who can be said to have formulated them" (p. 95). This comment from Foucault led Dreyfus and Rabinow (1982) to remark, in words also worth reproducing: "This is the insight, and this is the problem. How to talk about intentionality without a subject, a strategy without a strategist. The answer must lie in the practices themselves" (p. 187).

The practices in our case are the discourses of Wild Realism, as well as their publication in the specific magazines under examination. However, while these are practices that emerged from somewhere—they have a history—and certainly involved the intentions of actors at some point, like many practices they have "escaped the actors' intentions, as well as those of anybody else" (Dreyfus and Rabinow 1982: 187). Again, returning to

Foucault's words "People know what they do; they frequently know why they do what they do; but what they don't know is what what they do does" (Foucault quoted in ibid.). While authors of Wild Realist texts may be aware of the realist foundations of their assumptions, and may even consciously choose a vaguely realist approach, they are likely not aware that their theoretical assumptions or attempts to expunge theory from their writings, have certain effects. And whether they are aware of any of this or not, the discourse itself—their texts—still have effects beyond whatever the author did or did not intend for their texts to do (cf. Crapanzano's (2001) investigation of literalism).

Recalling the earlier discussion of multivocality and reflexivity, our approach to selecting empirical material is critical—not quantitative. We have not set out to analyse every magazine article from the Foreign Policy Commentariat. This book's critical discourse approach is post-positivist rather than positivist: it conceptualizes ontology and epistemology as being related, rather than being separate.[2] We can also think of this in terms of omni and multivocality. If we break texts down into words, do these words only have one fixed meaning (cf. omnivocality) or are they representative of numerous relationships (including grammar, history, and contexts) and interpretations based on these relationships (cf. multivocality)? In a critical discourse analysis, since ontology and epistemology are theorized as being related, reality (ontology) is conceptualized as being created through the way we know it (epistemology) (Fierke 2004: 36). This is not to deny the existence of a physical or material world, but is instead to claim we can only know it through human constructed knowledge—language, practices, etc.—that are themselves rooted in history and context (ibid.).

According to our methodology, if we were to attempt a quantitative analysis—to essentially count the number of relevant words in a set of data (i.e. all 8410 texts published in FP and FA between January 2008 and September 2024), we would be isolating these words from their context (Fierke 2004: 36). This context—the relationships and patterns of relationships between words—is what we are analysing, rather than the individual words themselves (cf. Doty 1993: 302). We aim to identify a

---

[2] Such separation is the case in many realist theories where ontology is taken to be objective reality, while epistemology is assumed to be formulated based on this entirely separate ontology. In other words, it is assumed there is a real world that can be objectively observed using universal laws (universal because the ontology is unchanging).

discourse of Wild Realism, and to then determine its effects and significance within the text of the Foreign Policy Commentariat. However, this does not mean that Wild Realism is the most prevalent discourse in these texts. Rather, Wild Realism's analytical value is in its situation between multiple different discourses and approaches, which allows us to focus on key points where multiple concepts are formulated or effaced (cf. Hansen 2006: 46–7; also see: 'intertextuality' in Doty 1993: 302, *et passim*).

THEORY: AN INTERSECTIONAL APPROACH

In this section we explain the theoretical framework used to problematize and understand how the Wild Realism discourse functions in the FPC texts, particularly in terms of power/knowledge.[3] Gender and postcoloniality are *intersectional*. What does it mean for identities (or concepts) to intersect? In the simplest formulation, this means that they interact, compound, exacerbate, and change the experiences and understandings of each other. In terms of identity, a white cis-gender woman will have different lived experiences compared to those of a cis-gender woman of colour. Being a person of colour will bring with it certain effects that will further shape their experience as a woman. This is of course a simplified example. In practice, there are a multitude of intersecting identities and factors that affect individuals' lived experiences.

The same underlying idea applies to analysis as well. Universalist approaches can obscure nuance and difference, which can in turn inhibit analysis. As Hudson (2005) points out, even using seemingly gender-neutral concepts such as 'human' (as in 'human security' or 'human rights') that collapse femininity and masculinity into one term runs the risk on concealing gendered practices (p. 157). Often, such terms are really an expression of masculinity (ibid.). And in practice, things are even more complicated. Gender, and all of the other identities it is intertwined with, is reproduced through processes that are local, regional, and global (ibid.). Indeed, just the concept of gender itself can be challenging to unpack.

Even if gender is understood as being a social construct, there is still the matter of the gendered subject. There is also the conceptually difficult matter of nailing down what counts as a gendered experience. There are,

---

[3] For Foucault there is no disinterested knowledge, knowledge and power are "inextricably interdependent" (Smart 2002: 58).

broadly, three approaches here: empiricist, standpoint, and poststructuralist feminism (Hansen 2010: 18; Harding 1986; Weber 1994). Empiricist or rationalist feminism assumes an unproblematic, biological divide between men and women. Essentially, this approach treats men and women as empirical categories (Hansen 2010: 19–20). This approach overlaps with rationalist, empiricist IR frameworks, and we see its expression most often in quantitative studies (e.g. do levels of equality affect states going to war? how many women are involved in peace processes? etc.), as well as comparative studies (ibid., pp. 20–1).

Standpoint feminism, rather than taking the universalist approach of rationalist feminism, does not view femininity and masculinity as uniform constructs, which are unchanging across time and space. Nor does this approach assume that women or men have inherent traits, e.g. tendencies to be peaceful or violent (Hansen 2010: 22). Standpoint feminism also maintains that there is a concrete female subject that can be referred to and who should be centred in analysis (ibid.). Poststructuralist feminism, on the other hand, takes a different approach. This approach does not conceptualize an extra-discursive biological gender—i.e. in this view gender is only constructed through discourse, rather than there being a 'biological gender' (Hansen 2010: 24). Instead, poststructuralist feminism relies on Judith Butler's concept of performativity: gender is something that is done, something that is always doing and being created through various practices (ibid.; see: Butler 2010).

Of course, there is a tension here. Essentially, it is this: we know that there is an identity of woman, but through knowing it (and describing or defining it so we can study it), are we merely reproducing gendered practices? Put more simply, if we want to put women or their experiences at the centre of our analysis, what definition of woman should we use? How do we decide which experiences are feminine and which are not? If we decide they all are, does this collapse the identity of woman? Indeed, as Hansen (2010) points out, the point of a poststructuralist approach is that discourses can silence and legitimate, which necessitates the need for a discourse analysis in the first place (p. 24). Regardless, this tension remains, though it is not necessarily a problem that needs to be (or can be) 'solved'. Again, gender is interwoven with (the production of) other identities. Particularly in the case of IR, through asking which different ways we can look at the world, we can help uncover how these overlapping identities are reproduced (sometimes through our own practices as analysts). In this way, we can attempt to connect individual experiences in particular locations to wider regional and global processes (Hudson 2005: 158).

* * *

How does this relate to an analysis of the Foreign Policy Commentariat's discourse? Our analysis does not focus on the number of women contributors to these magazines, or the topics which they commentate on (i.e. an empiricist approach). Based on our reading of FA and FP articles there are valid concerns as to gender balance which offer a potentially fruitful avenue for future quantitative research. However, we felt that determining which authors identify as women based solely on names could be both difficult and potentially quite problematic. We are moreover not implying that any of the writers under examination deliberately excluded women or gender from their articles. However, a gender/feminist approach can help us understand power (and knowledge) and how it is reproduced discursively.

Here we return to Butler's concept of performativity. In the standpoint feminist conceptualization, gender is theorized as a construct inscribed on bodies through social practices. In other words, there are bodies with biological sexes (male/female) who are gendered through processes that vary across time and space—'biological' females and males are coded through gendered language, practices, customs, etc. In Butler's performativity, sex is conceptualized as an *effect* of gender discourse, and the concepts of sex/gender are theorized as being co-constituted and inseparable (Weber 1998: 79). Part of what gives gender its ability to make authoritative statements (about inherent traits, etc.) is its claim to be based on the objective, pre-discursive fact of sex. What Butler argues, is that gender discourses construct the idea that sex is 'natural', pre-discursive, and pre-cultural, every time it is performed (ibid.). Through constructing its own natural, pre-discursive foundation, gender discourse is able to make a claim to a universal, inherent objectivity.

This is important for our analysis because gender is interwoven with and reflective of other practices used to construct and condition subjects. In traditional IR approaches, and especially in the Wild Realist discourse observed in the text of the FPC, states are understood as the ontological units under analysis. These states are then knowable and observable from a detached, scientific perspective. Of course, states do have a 'real' existence—we know their borders and their systems of governments. However, understanding how they (will) interact with each other can be a difficult proposition given their complexity. Furthermore, states, despite their tangible impacts, are also constructed conceptual tools used to make sense of numerous interactions at different scales. This is especially true for the conceptualisation of states as unitary rational actors. IR has developed concepts and theories over the years to understand how states work. Some of these approaches treat the state as enduring, universal units, and sometimes acting according to allegedly inherent human traits.[4] As these approaches are practiced, they perpetuate the concept of an ontological, universal, enduring state. In a sense, the epistemology produces the ontology through claiming its ontological status (its 'realness').

One way that different approaches to IR—especially realisms—have tried to understand how states behave is through the concept of 'anarchy'. Simply put, states are theorized as existing in anarchy. Without any overarching authority to control or order states, they behave in certain ways. There are many ways in which anarchy is conceptualized as affecting states across different theoretical approaches—the anarchy 'myths' (or the mythologization of realities of international anarchy) as Weber (2010: 14) puts it.[5] A common philosophical touchstone for theories that use anarchy as a concept, again particularly realisms, is the work of Thomas Hobbes—especially the 'state of nature' concept.[6]

The jump from Hobbes' state of nature to international anarchy seems straightforward. Hobbes argued that before the existence of government, people ("men" in his parlance) existed in a state of nature. In this state of nature, life was "solitary, poor, nasty, brutish, and short": people essentially just survived and there was very little beyond raw strength (of body or mind) to keep people from doing whatever they wanted.[7] Anarchy is

---

[4] These conceptualizations are not relegated to traditional positivist approaches in IR. As Campbell (2001) observes in Wendtian constructivism: "Wendt's conception of state centrism as being equivalent to the idea of the human body as the presocial foundation for human relations means that he has a state-centric theory that argues that states *really are* anthropomorphic, unitary actors, something that is more fixed than most formulations of realism that treat states *as though they were* actors of this kind" (p. 441, emphasis original).

[5] Weber (2010) provides a good overview of how these myths are used in realisms (pp. 13–36).

[6] As Williams (1996) quotes Michael Smith (1986): "analysis of the state of nature remains the defining feature of realist thought. His notion of the international state of nature as a state of war is shared by virtually everyone calling himself a realist."

[7] See Hobbes *Leviathan*.

conceptualized in similar terms: states, like people in the state of nature, are unconstrained by a Leviathan-like government and thus will behave like people concerned only with survival. However, a closer reading of Hobbes complicates this use of the state of nature.

In IR, the English School's 'rationalist' approach questioned why Hobbes himself never applied the state of nature concept to the international realm. That is, why did Hobbes not advocate a Leviathan government for the world as well? Their answer was that Hobbes did not see international relations and the state of nature as being directly analogous (Williams 1996: 214). Williams (1996) sees Hobbes' thought as being even more nuanced and sophisticated. For Williams (1996), Hobbes did not strictly base his analysis on "empirical facts or upon the straightforward rational calculations of rational actors responding to the objective conditions in which they find themselves" (p. 230). Nor was his Leviathan proposal an extension of laws of human nature based upon self-interest (and self-preservation) (ibid.). Instead, the Leviathan solved more complicated problems concerning epistemology and ethics (ibid.). Furthermore, within the Leviathan, (particularly when dealing with issues of international relations) the sovereign is careful not to lose the trust of his citizens. These domestic considerations mean that for Hobbes the state of nature is not completely resolved through the Leviathan—thus, contrary to (neo) realism, the state is not analogous to the individual in the state of nature, as it is a corporate body (ibid., p. 232).

Butler uses performativity to understand the discursive processes at work within the application of the anarchy concept. A state of nature discourse constructs a nonhistorical time before the 'foundation' of states/governments—in Butler's (2010) words it creates a "presocial ontology of persons who freely consent to be governed and, thereby, constitute the legitimacy of the social contract" (p. 4). The creation of this time 'before' is constituted by such discourse (and indeed through law) "as the fictive foundation of its own claim to legitimacy" (ibid.). This of course echoes the sex/gender performative processes described earlier, as well as how some approaches' epistemology constructs its own ontologies. We also arrive again at intersectionality. Beyond our identities, we are constantly reproduced and constructed as subjects before the law, represented by our state, etc.

When we examine a discourse like the Wild Realism of the FPC, we are not just looking at words. We are also observing the reproduction of particular forms of knowledge. This might not be explicit—indeed the rules for how knowledge should be disciplined are often immanent within discourse. So, we are examining what was 'said' as well as the rules that explain how it becomes possible to say (or know) what was said (Bacchi and Bonham 2014: 180). Also, these discourses are more than just writings in magazines. They are practices—the practice of analysing foreign policy and the practice of expertise, by experts in well-read and well-known publications (cf. ibid., p. 182; Foucault 2002). As we have seen, writing about concepts such as anarchy or states as unitary, rational actors reproduces more than just concepts themselves—there is an underlying knowledge, rules for how knowledge should be performed, and a claim to authority.

For example, when theories, such as realisms in IR, make the claim to understand how states behave using concepts not shaped by language—i.e. universal, unchanging ontologies—this is a claim to authority. Though not explicit, this approach implicitly silences the possibility of a framework that incorporates an analysis of language or discourse through denying its legitimacy. Furthermore, recalling Hobbes, the distinction between a stable, ordered domestic realm vs a domain of international anarchy where traditionally masculine traits of violence, power, and domination rule is a both a gendered practice in and of itself, and also recalls the public/private sphere distinction which structures many gendered/gendering discourses (Tickner 1988: 432).

This is clear in the writing of the FPC which broadly presupposes the existence of an international system, often referred to as a postwar or American led international system. Authors from different political affiliations and professional backgrounds, often with different policy advice, agree on this. However, it is not clear to the reader whether the international systems to which these authors refer actually overlap, and their key features have to be inferred from context as they are not clearly elucidated. The submerged nature of this assumption about the nature of reality allows the idea of an international system to function as a foundation for many different policy platforms and political interests. The idea of an international system is frequently invoked in FA and FP, whether it is postwar (Ikenberry 2019), post-Cold War (Krastev and Leonard 2015), world (Brzezinski 2010; Bacevich 2010), global (Haass 2021; Theil et al. 2024), American-led (Ikenberry 2022), liberal (Ikenberry 2020; Lind and Wohlforth 2019; Drezner 2019), rules-based (Rodrik and Walt 2022; Stuenkel 2024), hollow (Zelikow 2022), multipolar (Economy 2024; Rose 2019; Dickinson 2009), unipolar, bipolar (Xuetong 2019) or even non-polar (Haass 2008). The assumption that an international system exists is in itself a theoretical abstraction which seeks to make sense of a complex web of interactions at different scales and on different time-frames. This assumption is then reified through repetition, forming a basic feature of the worldview of those writing in FP and FA. "What do you mean by the international system?" may seem the kind of pointless philosophical question which is best kept away from a public facing and policy relevant publication. However, this underplays the explanatory power of theoretical concepts in making our world comprehensible, and the importance of communicating differences between these concepts to the public.

In addition to assuming the existence of an international system, the widespread adoption of this terminology makes authors' conceptions of this system seem more similar than they really are. This is particularly the case for the assumed general audience who have no reason to know their Wallersteins from their Walts or Wohlforths. Wallerstein's *'capitalist world economy'* is not the same international system as Rodrik and Walt's *'international order'* (Wallerstein 2011; Rodrik and Walt 2022). Yet when they write for FA and/or FP they use similar language to describe quite different understandings of an international system made up of interactions occurring at different scales. Many of the cited authors would be acutely aware of this and could provide interesting accounts of their conceptual choices. However, the lack of space offered by FP and FA to explain such choices, and indeed their editorial guidelines which push authors away from doing so, submerges differences between conceptualisations and closes down space for thinking about the 'international' differently.

In the Wild Realist discourse in the texts of the FPC, these issues become even more pronounced. In the realm of academic publishing, there are avenues for these approaches to be problematized. Even when such concepts as anarchy are not directly challenged, they are, for the most part, employed as concepts rather than ontological facts. The magazines in which the FPC publish limit the ability of these discourses to engage with the constructedness of their concepts. The reasons for this appear to be threefold. First, the editorial policies of FA and FP discourage discussions of theory. Second, and likely related to the first, these magazines overwhelmingly feature analysis that broadly mirrors realist, or at least traditionalist, approaches to IR. As such, these magazines do not attract academics who use different theoretical approaches (though there are many other reasons for this, including that these magazines are not peer-reviewed). There is also a third issue: realist approaches value parsimonious, 'scientific' accounts. Part of these approaches' claim to authority is their purported ability to understand 'real' issues objectively. Thus, the type of stripped back, theory-light writing that is present in FP and FA is conducive to broadly realist approaches.

*　*　*

We can further see the importance of problematizing universalization in the context of intersectionality. In the (western) academic literature, even up until the 1980s there was a tendency to assume that the political project of feminism was universal—that women across the world faced the same forms of oppression (McEwan 2001: 96). However, encounters with postcolonialist approaches challenged this universalism. It was not so much that feminist/gender studies scholars were actively ignoring the experiences and knowledge of non-western women (though this likely happened as well). Rather, the epistemological frameworks upon which these western feminist approaches were based lacked the ability to recover and understand the cultural and historical meanings of women's experiences in locations outside the west (ibid., p. 97; Mohanty 1988).

Such universalistic claims—about a universal female identity or universal patriarchy—are based on a common or shared epistemological standpoint (Butler 2010: 19). Rather than being universal, however, such claims about the universality of a female/woman identity (and what it is defined against) might itself be based on normative and exclusionary practices that do not account for the multiple intersecting practices through which 'women' are constructed (ibid). Seeking to include 'other' cultures (i.e. non-western ones) as also being oppressed by a universal patriarchy, risks "colonizing under the sign of the same those differences that might otherwise call that totalizing concept into question" (ibid., p. 18; see also: Spivak 1987).

Again, this is not necessarily an intentional strategy to marginalize the experiences of women from non-western locations. The construction of a universal patriarchy allowed feminism to strengthen its claim to be representative of all women. However, these particular universal constructs also meant that some types of feminist theorizing "colonize[d] and appropriate[d] non-Western cultures to support highly Western notions of oppression" (Butler 2010: 5). In this way these theories constructed a 'Third World' or an 'Orient' where gender oppression was explained, not in terms of local historical and cultural context, but instead as symptomatic of being non-western—especially in terms of a non-western 'barbarism' (ibid.). These moves were, in Butler's terms, part of an "colonizing epistemological strategy" that subordinated different configurations of domination and oppression to a universalized patriarchy (ibid., p. 48).

These epistemological strategies were produced through historical understanding in western academia that there was a 'duty' to represent the entire world—which itself is predicated on an authority to do so (McEwan 2001: 101). However, gender, feminist, and postcolonial scholarship has since reoriented western feminisms to recognize that there is a plurality of feminisms. These feminisms, as well as concepts of women, have their own history, locations, and political objectives. Furthermore, it is recognized that feminism does not originate in the west (ibid., p. 97). In this sense, such approaches have to transcend the colonizing practices and boundaries within modernist discourses (ibid., p. 101). Indeed, this recalls the discussions earlier in this chapter about the tension between conceptualizations of 'women', and of Hobbes and foundations of legitimacy. Conceptualizations—e.g. anarchy—can calcify into 'facts' without recognition of their constructed and historically contingent nature (even in academia). Through this reification, the processes that reconstruct such concepts (and their effects) continue to function but are occluded by the assumption that they are ontological facts.

Mohanty (1988) describes colonization as almost invariably implying a "relation of structural domination, and a discursive or political suppression of the heterogeneity of the subject(s) in question" (p. 61). Reflected in this definition is the above discussion about earlier feminist approaches that universalized women and the patriarchy—though without the structural dimension. This also indicates the insidious and pervasive nature of colonizing practices and of their constructions of power and authority. This is why a reflexive, critical approach is needed as a means of intervention into hegemonic discourses, whether they be political, practical, and/ or academic (ibid., p. 62).

CONCLUSION

This book utilizes these intersecting theories for different purposes in our empirical chapters. We use an intersectional gender and postcolonial approach to understand power and the performance of expertise in the discourse of the FPC. These texts are full of constructions of power and knowledge of how the international system works (itself predicated on the existence of an international system, which these discourses further reproduce).The discourse in these texts reproduces a particular US-centric viewpoint and foreign policy pronouncements that are imbricated with processes that discipline both knowledge of the world of foreign policy and what is appropriate US foreign policy leadership (or even what is appropriately American leadership).

In the following chapters, we use these theories to understand the functioning of the Wild Realism discourses in these texts. In particular, we are concerned with the construction of power/knowledge, with the understanding that the two are inextricably linked. In this Foucauldian understanding, knowledge does not detach itself "from its empirical roots, the initial needs from which it arose, to become pure speculation, subject only to the demands of reason" (Foucault quoted in Smart 2002: 58). Instead, knowledge is intertwined with power relations and advances in knowledge are imbricated with developments in the exercise of power (ibid.). As such, the sites where power is exercised are also where knowledge is produced, and vice versa (ibid.).

The enlightenment notions of rationality on which positivist approaches based are often rooted in older works—such as Hobbes—which reproduce a gendered understanding of politics, and thus international relations (Campbell 1998: 66). These understandings are predicated on hierarchies and dichotomies: strong/weak, public/private, rational/irrational, order/disorder, stability/anarchy, etc. (ibid.). Historically, gender has been mapped onto these dichotomies (and vice versa), with the first term identified with the masculine and the second with the feminine—and these notions have permeated understandings of international relations and foreign policy (ibid.).[8]

Not only can gendered understandings help us unpack power/knowledge, but so too can an intersecting postcolonial approach. Such an approach helps understand the above knowledge as contingent and contextual—it comes from a particular historical place with its attendant processes of power and understanding. Even advancing understandings—in claiming an authority to know how something works, across contexts—can be an exercise of power (though not necessarily intentionally). We can see this in the above discussion about how certain feminist theorizations ran the risk of homogenizing and thus effacing experience and knowledge in non-western contexts (cf. Butler 1994: 165).

---

[8] See also Ashley's (1989) explanation of the 'paradigm of sovereignty' for a further account of how these dichotomies have structured knowledge, as well as Ashley (1988).

REFERENCES

Ashley RK (1988) Untying the Sovereign State: A Double Reading of the Anarchy Problematique: *Millennium.* https://doi.org/10.1177/0305829888017 0020901

Ashley RK (1989) 'Living on Border Lines: Man, Poststructuralism, and War' in: Der Derian J and Shapiro MJ (eds) *International/Intertextual Relations: Postmodern Readings of World Politics.* Issues in world politics series. Lexington, Mass.: Lexington Books.

Bacchi C and Bonham J (2014) Reclaiming discursive practices as an analytic focus: Political implications. *Foucault Studies* 0(17): 179–192.

Andrew J. Bacevich, 'Let Europe Be Europe', *Foreign Policy,* no. 178 (3 April 2010): 71–72.

Zbigniew Brzezinski, 'From Hope to Audacity', *Foreign Affairs* 89, no. 1 (1 February 2010): 16–30.

Butler J (1994) Contingent foundations: Feminism and the question of 'postmodernism'. In: Seidman S (ed.) *The Postmodern Turn: New Perspectives on Social Theory.* Cambridge: Cambridge University Press, pp. 153–170.

Butler J (2010) *Gender Trouble: Feminism and the Subversion of Identity.* New York: Routledge.

Campbell D (1998) *Writing Security: United States Foreign Policy and the Politics of Identity.* Revised edition. Manchester: Manchester University Press.

Campbell D (2001) International Engagements: The Politics of North American International Relations Theory. *Political Theory* Gilbert A, Krasner S, and Wendt A (eds) 29(3). Sage Publications, Inc.: 432–448.

Crapanzano V (2001) *Serving the Word: Literalism in America from the Pulpit to the Bench.* New Press.

Elizabeth Dickinson, 'New Order', *Foreign Policy,* no. 175 (11 December 2009): 29–29.

Doty RL (1993) Foreign Policy as Social Construction: A Post-Positivist Analysis of U.S. Counterinsurgency Policy in the Philippines. *International Studies Quarterly* 37(3): 297–320.

Dreyfus HL and Rabinow P (1982) *Michel Foucault: Beyond Structuralism and Hermeneutics.* Brighton, England: Harvester.

Daniel W. Drezner, 'This Time Is Different: Why U.S. Foreign Policy Will Never Recover', *Foreign Affairs* 98, no. 3 (5 June 2019): 10–17.

Elizabeth Economy, 'China's Alternative Order: And What America Should Learn From It', *Foreign Affairs* (New York, United Kingdom: Council on Foreign Relations NY, June 2024).

Fierke KM (2004) Whereof We Can Speak, Thereof We Must Not Be Silent: Trauma, Political Solipsism and War. *Review of International Studies* 30(4): 471–491.

Foucault M (1980) *Power/Knowledge: Selected Interviews and Other Writings, 1972–1977* (ed. C. Gordon). Brighton: Harvester Press.

Foucault M (2002) *The Archaeology of Knowledge*. London: Routledge.

Richard N. Haass 'The Age of Nonpolarity', *Foreign Affairs*, 3 May 2008, https://www.foreignaffairs.com/articles/united-states/2008-05-03/age-nonpolarity

Richard Haass, 'The Age of America First', *Foreign Affairs* 100, no. 6 (11 December 2021): 85–98.

Hansen L (2006) *Security as Practice: Discourse Analysis and the Bosnian War*. New international relations. London: Routledge.

Hansen L (2010) 'Ontologies, Epistemologies, Methodologies' in: Shepherd LJ *Gender Matters in Global Politics: A Feminist Introduction to International Relations*. Florence, UNITED STATES: Taylor & Francis Group. Available at: http://ebookcentral.proquest.com/lib/st-andrews/detail.action?docID=481144

Harding SG (1986) *The Science Question in Feminism*. Milton Keynes: Open University Press.

Hudson H (2005) 'Doing' Security As Though Humans Matter: A Feminist Perspective on Gender and the Politics of Human Security. *Security Dialogue* 36(2): 155–174.

John Ikenberry, 'Enduring Alliance: A History of NATO and the Postwar Global Order', *Foreign Affairs* 98, no. 6 (11 December 2019): 200–200.

G. John Ikenberry, 'The Next Liberal Order', *Foreign Affairs* 99, no. 4 (7 August 2020): 133–42.

G. John Ikenberry, 'Why American Power Endures: The U.S.-Led Order Isn't in Decline', *Foreign Affairs* 101, no. 6 (11 December 2022): 56–73.

Ivan Krastev and Mark Leonard, 'Europe's Shattered Dream of Order', *Foreign Affairs* 94, no. 3 (5 June 2015): 48–58.

Jennifer Lind and William C. Wohlforth, 'The Future of the Liberal Order Is Conservative: A Strategy to Save the System', *Foreign Affairs* 98, no. 2 (3 April 2019): 70–80.

McEwan C (2001) Postcolonialism, feminism and development: intersections and dilemmas. *Progress in Development Studies* 1(2). Sage Publications, Ltd.: 93–111.

Mohanty CT (1988) Under Western Eyes: Feminist Scholarship and Colonial Discourses. *Feminist Review* (30). Sage Publications, Ltd.: 61–88.

Neal AW (2019) *Security as Politics: Beyond the State of Exception*. Edinburgh scholarship online. Edinburgh: University Press.

Dani Rodrik and Stephen M. Walt, 'How to Build a Better Order', *Foreign Affairs* 101, no. 5 (9 October 2022): 142–55.

Gideon Rose, 'Who Will Run the World?', *Foreign Affairs* 98, no. 1 (1 February 2019): 8–8.

Smart B (2002) *Michel Foucault*. Revised edition. London: Routledge.

Spivak GC (1987) *In Other Worlds: Essays in Cultural Politics*. Methuen.

Oliver Stuenkel, 'The Global South Is Accusing America of Hypocrisy', *Foreign Policy*, no. 251 (Winter 2024): 30–32.

Stefan Theil et al., 'Can Europe Fend for Itself?', *Foreign Policy*, no. 253 (Summer 2024): 34–49.

Tickner J. (1988) Hans Morgenthau's Principles of Political Realism: A Feminist Reformulation. *Millennium—Journal of International Studies* 17(3): 429–440.

Immanuel Wallerstein, 'The Global Economy Won't Recover, Now or Ever', *Foreign Policy*, no. 184 (1 February 2011): 76–76.

Weber C (1994) Good Girls, Little Girls, and Bad Girls: Male Paranoia in Robert Keohane's Critique of Feminist International Relations. *Millennium* 23(2). SAGE Publications Ltd: 337–349.

Weber C (1998) Performative States. *Millennium* 27(1): 77–95.

Weber C (2010) International Relations Theory: A Critical Introduction Cynthia Weber. Third edition. Milton Park, Abingdon, Oxon; Routledge.

Williams MC (1996) Hobbes and International Relations: A Reconsideration. *International Organization* 50(2): 213–236.

Williams MC (2005) *The Realist Tradition and the Limits of International Relations.* Cambridge Studies in International Relations; no. 100. Cambridge: Cambridge University Press.

Yan Xuetong, 'The Age of Uneasy Peace: Chinese Power in a Divided World', *Foreign Affairs* 98, no. 1 (1 February 2019): 40–46.

Philip Zelikow, 'The Hollow Order: Rebuilding an International System That Works', *Foreign Affairs* 101, no. 4 (7 August 2022): 107–19.

CHAPTER 3

US Foreign Policy Commentary in the Obama Era (2009–2017)

Abstract This chapter examines the FPC's discourse during the Obama administration. The FPC's assessments of President Obama's foreign policy are analyzed through a gender lens. Gendered constructs are observed in the FPC's Wild Realism discourse that were used to discipline and reinforce assumptions about how a US president should conduct foreign policy. In particular, this analysis interrogates gendered constructs of strength/weakness in the Wild Realism discourse.

Keywords Obama • Syria • Gender • Masculinity • Idealized president • Weakness • Credibility

During the administration of President Obama, the FPC's discourse was overall critical both of Obama's foreign policy and his leadership. Many of the critiques in the pages of *Foreign Affairs* (FA) and *Foreign Policy* (FP) were focused on the alleged 'weakness' or indecisiveness of the Obama foreign policy. The concept of credibility was also invoked, which was inherently tied to Obama as a personification of the US, as well as a further reconstruction of a gendered strength/weakness dichotomy.

However, this discourse is more than just foreign policy experts calling a sitting president and his foreign policy weak. These pronouncements are based on a presumed authority to pronounce on what appropriate (US)

© The Author(s), under exclusive license to Springer Nature Switzerland AG 2025
D. Mobley, J. Gazeley, *Understanding Foreign Policy Commentary*,
https://doi.org/10.1007/978-3-031-95473-3_3

31

foreign policy should look like, as well as how a president should conduct themselves. This is quite a claim to authority, in that it presumes to know what is acceptably American (in terms of being true to some innate American-ness, and what is in the best interests of the US), as well as how the international system functions. Identifying this construction of authority is not to pass judgement on these commentators or their assessments—most of them do have expert knowledge, through practice and research, about many aspects of US foreign policymaking, as well as world politics. However, the performance of this expertise in these texts, particularly when drawing on unproblematized theoretical concepts, does produce a claim to knowledge and thus exerts power.

Through assessing the Obama presidency, the FPC defined not only a particular conceptualization of an idealized president—strong, firm, decisive, rational, credible—but also reproduced specific, accepted ways of understanding presidents and foreign policies. The order of the state and a US-led international system were set against anarchy; a rational US state actor was constructed as the point from which analysis was made; and was further constructed as a rational, ordered site of knowledge. In turn, the US and its responsibilities were constructed as powerful and important in an anarchic world looking for leadership and safety in order. This understanding of the US was then personified in the form of an ideal US president, against which Obama was defined.

*   *   *

The President Obama presented in the discourse of the FPC, from early in his presidency to the very end of his second term, is a foreign policy chameleon. This appears to reflect that this former senator with little prior foreign policy experience was something of a blank slate upon which various authors could project their fears and hopes. But despite the lack of a clearly defined Obama Doctrine,[1] this period is still extremely valuable as a window into how the commentariat responded to his performance of foreign policy expertise through performances of their own.

A consistent theme in articles on the Obama foreign policy is the gap between rhetoric and action. Declining perceptions of Obama's foreign policy expertise are revealing as they demonstrate a growing realisation of

---

[1] Notwithstanding an article of this name, which mostly focused on the failures of Obama's approach to the War on Terror (Rohde 2012).

the gap, not merely between the rhetoric and action of one individual, but between Obama himself and the Foreign Policy Commentariat's idealised vision of how a US President should perform foreign policy. With few exceptions the foundations of this idealised vision of the presidential role are shaped by a Wild Realist worldview: the performance of power in service of the national interest by a decisive and rational singular decisionmaker.

Senator Obama appears to have worked hard to project an image of foreign policy competence, particularly on matters of war. Then candidate Obama received a daily briefing from a pool of 300 foreign policy advisers structured to mirror the US State Department (Bumiller 2008). This fact was apparently shared with the media in part to craft an image of thoughtful process at odds with the Bush years. This process-scaffolding to buttress Presidential decision-making continued in office. Under President Obama the National Security Council reached historic size. Writing in FP Brzezinski[2] commented favourably on Obama's willingness to take advice, but gestured towards the need to manage carefully the:

> [...] largest National Security Council in history-its over-200-person staff is almost four times as large as the NSC staffs of Richard Nixon, Jimmy Carter, and George H. W. Bush and almost ten times as large as John F Kennedy's. (Brzezinski 2010: 17)

This early in Obama's tenure Brzezinski was at pains to give him the benefit of the doubt. He emphasized that despite this strong group of advisers it was Obama who set the overall strategic direction. However, in his effort to give Obama the benefit of the doubt he also exposed some of the gap between his idealized vision of the Presidency and the office holder:

> Obama himself is the main source of the strategic direction, but, unavoidably, he is able to play this role on only a part-time basis. This is a weakness, because the conceptual initiator of a great power's foreign policy needs to be actively involved in supervising the design of the consequent strategic decisions, in overlooking their implementation, and in making timely adjustments. Yet Obama has had no choice but to spend much of his first year in office on domestic political affairs. (Brzezinski 2010: 17–8)

---

[2] An influential foreign policy commentator, former academic, former National Security Adviser to the Carter administration and previously an adviser to the Johnson administration.

34   D. MOBLEY AND J. GAZELEY

Brzezinski here is clearly invoking staples of realist thought with reference to Great Powers, and strategic individual leadership of foreign policy. The words 'part-time basis' sit uneasily with Wild Realist ideas of presidential leadership. Indeed, with hindsight, the level of performative foreign policy process and advice perhaps helped to prepare the ground for later perceptions of Obama as weak and indecisive. The FPC appear to have conceptualised the ideal President as a solitary figure, who must have the self-confidence to trust their own judgement, and who therefore has no need for teams of advisers or rigid processes. Already at this early stage Brzezinski is beginning to communicate the sense of drift which later became the overriding impression of the Obama presidency among the Commentariat. Writing in 2010 he attributed this to bureaucratic inertia holding back Obama's attempts at radicalism:

> As a result, his grand redefinition of U.S. foreign policy is vulnerable to dilution or delay by upper-level officials who have the bureaucratic predisposition to favor caution over action and the familiar over the innovative. (Brzezinski 2010: 18)

Overall, Brzezinski (2010) presented a vision of a strong foreign policy held back by foreign influenced domestic lobbies, such as over Middle East policy and Israel, and by cautious or foot-dragging officials (p. 18). He also linked this to an over-involved legislature intruding on foreign policy, for example over Iran sanctions. (p. 29). Specifically, he pointed to polarisation and an ideological divide destroying the bipartisanship which foreign policy needs. Lest a reader in the 2020s should credit Brzezinski with an impressive foresight into the shape of US politics over the next decade he rather quaintly blamed the blogosphere for this (p. 29). More problematically, he exhibited some of the hauteur which Beltway insiders have too often displayed, and which contributes to political polarization and the ideological divide, in his claim that the US population is too ignorant and poorly informed to understand foreign policy issues, which he further contended has hamstrung policymaking in a large democracy (p. 30). Despite advancing these explanations for a perceived lack of progress, he did reserve some criticism for Obama himself, arguing that:

> [Obama] has not yet made the transition from inspiring orator to compelling statesman. Advocating that something happen is not the same as making it happen. (Brzezinski 2010: 30)

This implies that Brzezinski's vision of statesmanship is, at least in part, defined by the willingness and ability to impose one's will. This sense that Obama struggled to transition from campaign (advocating for a vision) to leadership (creating that vision) was not limited to Brzezinski. Indeed, an entire segment of the November issue of 2010, provocatively titled *Plan B*, was premised on the need for a series of FP contributors to reboot Obama's flagging presidency.[3] In the 2010 FP survey Obama scored only 6 out of 10 for his job performance, slipping from 7 out 10 the year before, and suggesting a softening of support amongst the commentariat (*Foreign Policy* 2010). There was a partisan element to this debate, with Republican leaning members of the Foreign Policy Commentariat outlining a narrative of persistent decline under his stewardship of the national interest. These contributors argued that Obama suffered from Carterism or from being a nice guy who just didn't have what it takes, i.e. the strength and decisive masculine rationality, to run a successful Foreign Policy. This declinist tendency presented Obama as weak, dithering and aloof as President.[4]

We can observe here overlapping concerns with foreign policy and national security, manifested in particularly gendered language. As is shown in the articles critical of the Obama foreign policy approach below, there is a clear prioritization of certain attributes and traits over others— not just by the FPC, but by the Obama administration as well. In US foreign policymaking, notions of national security (which like the national interest is subjective and constructed) have long been tied to military strength and the physical protection of the state from external threats (Tickner 1988: 435). This focus on external threats reproduces an inside/ outside dichotomy that recalls the realist assertion that the US is a site of order amidst a dangerous, disordered anarchic world. Attributes such as power, self-reliance, autonomy, and rationality are ones that both academic realist theories and the Wild Realist discourse consider desirable for a state (if that state is to survive this anarchical system). And indeed, these attributes are ones historically associated with a constructed 'ideal-type' masculinity (Tickner 2004: 44).

---

[3] This included contributions from: Nouriel Roubini, Michael Moran, Robert Shrum, R. James, Woolsey, Elliott Abrams, Bruce Riedel, Ellen Laipson, Will Marshall, James Hansen, Christopher Preble and Joseph Cirincione. (*Foreign Policy* 2010: 70–7).

[4] For example: Rove and Gillespie (2012), Nasr (2013) and Perle (2013).

Initially these critics were minority voices, outweighed by more hopeful interpretations. For example, the 2012 FA article "Scoring Obama's Foreign Policy" presented a mostly positive view (Indyk et al. 2012). However, even this relatively soft assessment concluded with a note of caution, and a rather backhanded defence, arguing that his critics had judged him unfairly by expecting signature achievements. The authors wrote that:

> Obama's foreign policy has been sensible and serious but not pathbreaking. It has stewarded the nation's interests competently in most areas, with few signature accomplishments (apart from the killing of Osama bin Laden) that might create a distinctive historical legacy… the gap between the president's rhetoric and his deeds has generated disappointment at home and abroad among those who did not appreciate that Obama's way of achieving progress is incremental rather than transformational. (Indyk et al. 2012: 42)

For FP and FA contributors the assassination of bin Laden was often invoked to set-up criticisms rather than discussed as a genuine foreign policy achievement (see Nasr 2013: 42). Outside the commentariat this assassination appears to have been deployed domestically as a sign of foreign policy expertise. Republican aligned commentators (Rove and Gillespie 2012) were not slow to point out that Obama mentioned Bin-Laden many more times in official speeches following the raid on Abbottabad than in all previous years combined (see Fig. 3.1).

The domestic implications of foreign policy actions appear to have been important for the Obama administration, and the developing impression of indecisiveness within the foreign policy commentariat by 2012 seems to have been considered a potential election weakness. For context, at this time the Obama administration was accused by critics from across the

Fig. 3.1 Graphic from an article in the March/April 2012 edition of FP by Rove and Gillespie (2012: 22) titled *How to Beat Obama*

political spectrum, from John McCain to Glenn Greenwald,[5] of leaking national security information to build Obama a tough-guy image. These critics pointed to suspiciously well-sourced articles in the New York Times[6] as well as support for the movie Zero Dark Thirty[7] and public revelation of the Stuxnet attack on the Iranian nuclear programme (Greenwald 2012).

Obama's reputation among the Foreign Policy Commentariat for weakness and indecisiveness, as developed within the pages of FP and FA, appears disconnected from the reality of his foreign policy record (and did not prevent him from winning a second term). It was also not how Obama was viewed across the political spectrum with scholars on the left, such as Perry Anderson who memorably referred to Obama as the 'Executioner in Chief' (2014: 108), constructing a more warlike and belligerent impression of his foreign policy leadership. This impression of willingness to use force, while articulated through hyperbole, appears to fit better with the underlying foreign policy empirical record. By 2014 President Obama had ordered airstrikes on at least seven countries[8] and authorised 542 drone strikes across his two terms in office.[9] On paper it is hard to imagine someone who more embodies Arthur Miller's description of the president who can both '*deliver the Sunday lesson*' and whose '*sword is never out of reach*' (Miller 2001: 80). In 2011, in a potentially apocryphal quote, Obama allegedly told aides:

Turns out I'm really good at killing people. Didn't know that was gonna be a strong suit of mine.[10]

Nevertheless, Obama's performance of a willingness to use force left the FPC unmoved.

The 2011 military intervention in Libya gained surprisingly little attention within the pages of FP and FA and was not directly dealt with as a question of Obama's foreign policy expertise. Indeed, this intervention was initially trumpeted as a success, only much later being re-interpreted as a foreign policy catastrophe. During his first address to the nation on the topic of the intervention in Libya Obama took full, personal,

---

[5] See for example: Dyer (2012) and Greenwald (2012).
[6] For example: Becker and Shane (2012).
[7] Which dramatized Operation Neptune's Spear, (the assassination of Osama Bin-Laden).
[8] According to CNN, see: Liptak (2014).
[9] According to the CFR, see: Zenko (2017).
[10] See: Zenko (2017) also see: Reilly (2013).

responsibility for an apparent mission accomplished. He argued that his decision to intervene was the right one, and that:

America has an important strategic interest in preventing Qaddafi from overrunning those who oppose him. A massacre would have driven thousands of additional refugees across Libya's borders, putting enormous strains on the peaceful – yet fragile – transitions in Egypt and Tunisia. The democratic impulses that are dawning across the region would be eclipsed by the darkest form of dictatorship, as repressive leaders concluded that violence is the best strategy to cling to power. The writ of the United Nations Security Council would have been shown to be little more than empty words, crippling that institution's future credibility to uphold global peace and security. So while I will never minimize the costs involved in military action, I am convinced that a failure to act in Libya would have carried a far greater price for America. (The White House 2011)

Contributors to FP and FA gave the administration significant leeway to frame the Libya intervention as a success. In an otherwise critical 2012 article, Rohde gave the Obama camp's view on Libya, reporting that:

Senior administration officials cite the toppling of Muammar al-Qaddafi as the prime example of the success of their more focused, multilateral approach to the use of force. At a cost of zero American lives and $1 billion in U.S. funding, the Libya intervention removed an autocrat from power in five months. The occupation of Iraq claimed 4,484 American lives, cost at least $700 billion, and lasted nearly nine years... "The light U.S. footprint had benefits beyond less U.S. lives and resources," [Ben] Rhodes [then Deputy National Security Advisor for Strategic Communications] told me. "We believe the Libyan revolution is viewed as more legitimate. The U.S. is more welcome. And there is less potential for an insurgency because there aren't foreign forces present." (Rohde 2012: 69)

With hindsight, the complacency of this view makes for painful reading. Yet the catastrophe in Libya took time to filter through to the FPC. Among this group, Libya was not cemented as a failure until the publication of an FA article in 2015 by Kuperman (2015) titled "Obama's Libya Debacle". The slowly unfolding horror, as it spread from Libya across the wider region, was matched by an attempt by the Obama administration to minimise responsibility and to pass as much blame as possible to the Europeans.[11]

---

[11] For example, see: Goldberg (2016).

This was, although not entirely unwarranted, perceived as unedifying behaviour and the phrase "leading from behind" (Rogin 2011) would come to dog his foreign policy legacy amongst the Commentariat, along with his most (in)famous, and autonymic, foreign policy maxim, "Don't do stupid shit" (Rothkopf 2014a).

Even before widespread recognition of the magnitude of the catastrophe in Libya, impressions of Obama's foreign policy performance were deteriorating. By 2013 FP was running multi-article features with titles such as "10 Problems Obama Actually Could Solve" (*Foreign Policy* 2013: 0–64). The suggestions given by the Commentariat on how to improve Obama's foreign policy in his second term range from prescient but hard to operationalise (save American democracy—Sifry), to cruel (get his authority back—Brzezinski), to, building on the successful raid on Abottabad which killed Osama Bin Laden, a reconceptualization of the role of the US President as something akin to a global bounty hunter (Get Kony—Prendergast).

From 2014 FP coverage adopted an increasingly pessimistic and critical tone. Even the (usually up-beat) editorial to the December 2014 issue was reduced to proclaiming "Disorder, not despair". This built on a 2014 article which asked whether Obama's foreign policy "could be saved?" (Rothkopf 2014b). Writing in FP in 2014 Rothkopf lambasted Obama for his failure to adapt, writing that:

> Obama seems steadfast in his resistance both to learning from his past errors and to managing his team so that future errors are prevented. It is hard to think of a recent president who has grown so little in office. (Rothkopf 2014b: 46)

At the root of Rothkopf's critique is Obama's perceived weakness and indecisiveness over the aborted 2013 air campaign in Syria. As the Syrian Civil War descended into brutality, with increasing evidence of crimes against humanity being perpetrated by the Syrian regime, Obama personally stated to assembled reporters that he would consider use of chemical weapons in Syria a red line, which would 'change his calculus' on intervention. For Rothkopf (and many other observers), the chemical weapons attack on Ghouta, a suburb of Damascus was a decisive moment. Rothkopf argues that:

The tripwire strung by the president himself had been clearly and unmistakably tripped. Now, his credibility was at stake. (Rothkopf 2014b: 46)

The language of credibility is interesting here, as it is not just the personal credibility of the President which was at stake, but the credibility of US foreign policy, and ultimately the nation itself. Seemingly a Cold War relic, the concept of credibility seems to have spread far beyond the ideas of containment and deterrence theory which it underpins (Huth 1988). This language is also present in Brzezinski's 2013 article, which does not specifically mention Syria and was written prior to the chemical attack in Ghouta, but followed a year of selective awareness (on the part of the Obama administration) of events in Syria which would seem to infringe the President's red line. In this article he exhorted Obama to "get his authority back" and "be a leader now" (Brzezinski 2013: 56).

Ultimately Obama was unwilling to use force in Syria and the moment passed with a fudged compromise. Russian President Vladimir Putin scored a diplomatic coup by negotiating the supposed destruction of Syrian chemical weapons stockpiles (Gordon 2013), further inserting Russia into the region and the conflict whilst the public climbdown damaged the Obama administration. As initial deployments of naval assets were underway, the US reached out to allies to gauge their willingness to participate in military operations against the Assad regime. The UK and France both signalled their readiness to join a relatively symbolic US punitive strike on targets in Syria. However, this plan unravelled quickly.

The British parliament voted against intervention in Syria, constraining the ability of Prime Minister David Cameron to contribute to an allied strike (*BBC News* 2013). Following this failed vote Obama made the decision not to go ahead without a vote in Congress. The strategic use of this vote in the British parliament to justify this course of (in)action further contributed to the sense that Obama was unable to make the big decisions, and further cemented the doubts amongst the Commentariat originated by his poorly chosen phrase 'leading from behind'[12] in the 2011 Libyan intervention. The decision to pull back, with allied (French) jets on the runway shattered the relationship between Obama and President François Hollande who has in subsequent years been open about his sense of betrayal.[13] Rothkopf's choice of quotes is instructive, helping him to

[12] Originally from an interview with the New Yorker, see: Lizza (2011).
[13] See: Davet and Lhomme (2016).

3 US FOREIGN POLICY COMMENTARY IN THE OBAMA ERA (2009–2017)   41

make the argument that the Ghouta incident was more than just a missed policy opportunity or an error, but was symptomatic of a failed foreign policy:

> "This was the real turning point for the administration's foreign policy," a former senior Obama advisor told me. "This was when things really started to go bad." (Rothkopf 2014b: 47)

Rothkopf gives no clues as to the identity of this adviser, or the level of first-hand involvement they had on foreign policy issues, but the overall impression which this quote is intended to create is clear. For Rothkopf, the decision demonstrated that Obama had let down his office through his failure to adequately perform foreign policy expertise. He dithered and exposed himself, and by extension his nation, as irresolute and sought to pass the buck to others. Of Obama's decision to go back to Congress for a vote authorising military action, Rothkopf (2014b) writes:

> It was clear from the outset that Congress would never approve the president's request and that, in asking for it, he was effectively seeking to be denied – as if to say, "Stop me before I take a risk I really don't want to take." It also set a precedent that would seemingly require the president to seek congressional approval for future military actions, even though the War Powers Resolution explicitly notes that he does not require it. (ibid., p. 47)

Brzezinski also shared this dim view of Obama's tendency to indecision, with his 2013 article advising him that:

> A president who aspires to be recognized as a global leader should not stake out a foreign-policy goal, commit himself eloquently to its attainment, and then yield the ground when confronted by firm opposition. (Brzezinski 2013: 56)

Both these critiques compare Obama to an ideal conceptualisation of the president, shaped to fit a Wild Realist worldview premised on the need for strength within an anarchic international system. This figure does not seek to pass the buck, to Congress, to the British parliament or to anyone else. Indeed, one of Obama's Democratic predecessors, and a contributor to the idealised vision of what a president should be, Harry S. Truman indelibly associated himself with this particular phrase with a sign on his

42   D. MOBLEY AND J. GAZELEY

desk reading 'The buck stops here!'.[14] This crystallises the central criticism of Obama's foreign policy performance. On the big calls, whether intervention in Libya or the aborted intervention in Syria, the critique from the FPC was not that Obama made the wrong one, but that he did not make one at all.

CONCLUSION

The Wild Realist worldview presupposes the material, observable and quantifiable existence of a national interest. Whilst the Commentariat disagrees vehemently over what this national interest is, they do agree that it exists and should orient foreign policy. Despite a relatively interventionist presidency, Obama was continually portrayed by the Foreign Policy Commentariat as weak and indecisive. His observable willingness to utilise force in pursuit of his articulation of the national interest (as in the case of intervention in Libya) did not matter to the Foreign Policy Commentariat for whom it seemed he could never go far enough. In this sense, the perceived failures to act decisively, such as during the Syrian Civil War, outweighed an otherwise evident willingness to use force.

The overriding impression of Obama, within the pages of FP and FA, was of a disjuncture between Obama's performance of individualised willingness to use force and a suspicion that underneath lay a more process-driven and consultative understanding of foreign policy expertise inimical to a Wild Realist worldview. Perhaps the apparent insincerity at the heart of the Obama project is what ultimately rendered it risible for the Foreign Policy Commentariat, or perhaps the nature of commentary itself leans more naturally towards critique than towards affirmation. In any case, the effort made by Obama early on to present a developed foreign policy framework and ambitious vision of change was undermined by the relatively small-scale of change actually contemplated when it came to delivery. Around the mid-point of the Obama era sympathetic commentators defended his first-term record on the grounds that "Obama's way of achieving progress is incremental rather than transformational" (Indyk et al. 2012), but this fell flat for most who felt that transformational change had been consistently promised.

The FPC's assessments of Obama and his administration's foreign policies reveal particular appraisals of power. The discourse, particularly

---

[14] See: https://www.trumanlibrary.gov/education/trivia/buck-stops-here-sign

regarding Syria, portrays Obama and his foreign policy as weak and indecisive. Though not explicit, these are nevertheless gendered constructions. The overall takeaway is that Obama should have been firm, strong, decisive—action should have been taken, for its own sake and for the sake of US credibility (presumably for action in the future). Furthermore, Syria is not portrayed as having any agency in the matter. Moreover, Syria as an actor (or really, object) is black-boxed. Arguably, the defining feature of the Syrian conflict was that it was a civil war. The internal dimension is overwhelmingly relevant, and the US was not simply dealing with another sovereign state.[15]

Such evaluations in the pages of these magazines, reproduce certain understandings. Yes, many of the commentators writing in these articles will have more nuanced views and assessments beyond these commentaries. However, the structural constraints of FP and FA and the type of Wild Realist discourse they promote (intentionally or otherwise), reinforced particular ways of knowing foreign policy and therefore reinforced both the authority to perform such expertise and reproduced certain ideas of US power and responsibility.

References

Anderson, P., (2014). *American Foreign Policy and Its Thinkers*, p.108.

BBC News (2013) Syria crisis: Cameron loses Commons vote on Syria action. 29 August. Available at: https://www.bbc.com/news/uk-politics-23892783

Becker J and Shane S (2012) Secret 'Kill List' Proves a Test of Obama's Principles and Will. *The New York Times*, 29 May. Available at: https://www.nytimes.com/2012/05/29/world/obamas-leadership-in-war-on-al-qaeda.html

Bumiller E (2008) Cast of 300 Advises Obama on Foreign Policy. *New York Times*, Jul 18. Available at: https://www.nytimes.com/2008/07/18/us/politics/18advisers.html?hp

Zbigniew Brzezinski, 'From Hope to Audacity', *Foreign Affairs* 89, no. 1 (1 February 2010): 16–30.

Zbigniew Brzezinski, Get His Authority Back, *Foreign Policy*, January/February 2013, No. 198.

---

[15] A similar approach was taken during the Trump administration regarding Iran, whose internal politics were of paramount importance in assessing the effectiveness and usefulness of the JCPOA. Conceptualizing Iran as a unitary actor was not helpful in this circumstance either.

Davet G and Lhomme F (2016) Le jour où... Obama a laissé tomber Hollande. 24 August. Available at: https://www.lemonde.fr/politique/article/2016/08/24/le-jour-ou-obama-a-laisse-tomber-hollande_4987167_823448.html

Dyer G (2012) Obama denies White House role in leaks. *Financial Times*, 8 June. Available at: https://www.ft.com/content/80cbeec8-b18a-11e1-9800-0014 4feabdc0

Foreign Policy, Plan B, November 2010, No. 182 (November 2010), Slate Group, LLC, pp. 70–77.

Foreign Policy, 10 Problems Obam Actually Could Solve, No. 198, January/February 2013, pp. 50–64.

Goldberg J (2016) The Obama Doctrine. *The Atlantic*, 10 March. Available at: https://www.theatlantic.com/magazine/archive/2016/04/the-obama-doctrine/471525/

Gordon MR (2013) U.S. and Russia Reach Deal to Destroy Syria's Chemical Arms. *The New York Times*, 14 September. Available at: https://www.nytimes.com/2013/09/15/world/middleeast/syria-talks.html

Greenwald G (2012) Tough Guy Leaking: Iran edition. *Salon*, Available at: https://www.salon.com/2012/06/01/tough_guy_leaking/ (accessed 15 January 2025).

Huth, P., (1988). *Extended Deterrence and the Prevention of War*. Yale University Press.

Indyk, Martin S.; Lieberthal, Kenneth G.; O'Hanlon, Michael E. Scoring Obama's Foreign Policy: A Progressive Pragmatist Tries to Bend History, *Foreign Affairs*, Vol. 91, Issue 3 (May/June 2012), pp. 29–42.

Alan J. Kuperman, *Foreign Affairs*, March/April 2015, Obama's Libya Debacle How a Well-Meaning Intervention Ended in Failure.

Liptak K (2014) Countries bombed by the U.S. under the Obama administration I CNN Politics. Available at: https://www.cnn.com/2014/09/23/politics/countries-obama-bombed/index.html

Lizza R (2011) An American President Abroad. *The New Yorker*, 25 April. Available at: https://www.newyorker.com/magazine/2011/05/02/the-consequentialist

Miller, A., (2001), On politics and the art of acting, Viking: NY.

Vali Nasr, 'My time in the Obama administration turned out to be a deeply disillusioning experience.": *Foreign Policy*, MARCH/APRIL 2013, No. 199 (MARCH/APRIL 2013), pp. 42–46, 48–51, Slate Group, LLC, https://www.jstor.org/stable/24575918

Richard Perle, Ditherer-in-Chief, *Foreign Policy*, JULY/AUGUST 2013, No. 201 (JULY/AUGUST 2013), pp. 12–13, Slate Group, LLC Stable https://www.jstor.org/stable/24575956

3 US FOREIGN POLICY COMMENTARY IN THE OBAMA ERA (2009–2017)   45

Reilly M (2013) Obama Reportedly Told Aides He's 'Really Good At Killing People'. *HuffPost UK*, 3 November. Available at: https://www.huffpost.com/entry/obama-drones-double-down_n_4208815

Rogin, 2011, Who really said Obama was "leading from behind"?—Foreign Policy.

Rohde, David. "The Obama Doctrine." Foreign Policy, no. 192 (2012): 64–69. http://www.jstor.org/stable/23237856

David Rothkopf, 2014a, June 4, 2014 Obama's 'Don't Do Stupid Shit' Foreign Policy—Foreign Policy.

David Rothkopf (2014b), National Insecurity, *Foreign Policy*, Sept/Oct 2014, No. 208, pp. 44–51, Slate Group, LLC, https://www.jstor.org/stable/24577435

Karl Rove and Ed Gillespie, How to Beat Obama, *Foreign Policy*, March / April 2012, No. 192 (March / April 2012), pp. 22–23, Slate Group, LLC, https://www.jstor.org/stable/23237844

The White House: Office of the Press Secretary, March 28, 2011, Remarks by the President in Address to the Nation on Libya, National Defense University, Washington, D.C.

Tickner J. (1988) Hans Morgenthau's Principles of Political Realism: A Feminist Reformulation. *Millennium—Journal of International Studies* 17(3): 429–440.

Tickner JA (2004) Feminist responses to international security studies. *Peace Review* 16(1). Routledge: 43–48.

Zenko M (2017) Obama's Final Drone Strike Data | Council on Foreign Relations. *Council of Foreign Relations*, 20 January. Available at: https://www.cfr.org/blog/obamas-final-drone-strike-data

CHAPTER 4

US Foreign Policy Commentary in the Trump Era (2017–2021)

Abstract This chapter unpacks the vaguely realist concepts used in the FPC's analyses of the first Trump administration, recognizing them as analytical concepts that are treated as ontologically given. This examination understands the FPC's appraisal of Trump's foreign policy—especially through the ontologisation of concepts—as hindered by a presumption that President Trump's domestic policy moves were articulations of a disruptive, yet coherent foreign policy that was a part of a broader trend of foreign policy sea change. The effects of reproducing concepts as ontological facts, rather than analytical tools, are interrogated in the chapter.

Keywords Trump • Rationality • National interest • Black box • Unitary actors

Perhaps unsurprisingly, much of the discourse about the Trump administration in FA and FP was centred on themes of 'aberration' from norms of foreign policy, as well as departures from 'establishment' thinking. However, while many of the authors—though not all—were seemingly uncomfortable with the Trump approach to foreign policy, there was disagreement about where these aberrations and departures took place. Regardless, throughout these texts there was a rather consistent theme of

© The Author(s), under exclusive license to Springer Nature Switzerland AG 2025
D. Mobley, J. Gazeley, *Understanding Foreign Policy Commentary*, https://doi.org/10.1007/978-3-031-95473-3_4

47

aberration from the norm of both foreign policymaking and of presidential leadership. Of course, there were many differences between the Trump administration and previous ones. However, the discourse in these texts conceptualized these changes in a rather narrow manner.

Overwhelmingly, the discourse of the FPC portrayed Trump as having a coherent foreign policy. While, certainly, this administration did have policies that dealt with international matters, there was not the same level of coherence as in previous administrations. Here again we see a conflation between the person of the president and the US as a (unitary) state. As the US was assumed to inherently have a foreign policy so too was Trump. The assessments of Trump are instructive in that they clearly demonstrate the tendency of these discourses to construct foreign policymaking as rational acts by rational actors, as a part of a cohesive doctrine enacted in aid of US national interests.

Rather than using concepts such as national interest, the international system, and state power as tools to understand the Trump's administration's actions and policies, these texts generally attempted to fit Trump into the concepts. Instead of interpreting Trump's actions and comments as domestic political moves that used the vocabulary of foreign policy, the FPC understood this discourse as a statement of foreign policy. As such, Trump's discourse was interpreted as an articulation of a disruptive, yet coherent foreign policy that was a part of a broader trend of foreign policy sea change, similar to other shifts in historical US foreign policy (particularly the change between Cold War and post-Cold War).

* * *

Writing in 2017, Elliot Abrams claimed that it had initially seemed "likely" that Trump would "represent a dramatic change" from traditional US foreign policy because of Trump's "apparent discomfort with the traditional role of 'leader of the free world'" (pp. 13–4). However, for Abrams (2017), this change initially occurred under Obama who "despite occasional rhetorical gestures, eschewed that role as well, casting doubt on U.S. commitments to democracy and human rights, especially in the Middle East" (p. 14). As such, Abrams (2017) thought it was "reasonable to expect that, in this regard, Trump would follow Obama's lead and would likely show even more indifference or hostility to policies based on intangible values such as international leadership, morality, and human rights" (ibid.). In Abrams' reading however, Trump performed the "surprising" move of launching cruise missiles in retaliation for chemical weapons attacks in Syria (ibid.). Indeed, for Abrams, this was what "most other modern presidents" would have also done—though not Obama, who would have, according to Abrams, dismissed such a retaliation as following the "Washington playbook" (ibid.). Interestingly, Abrams makes no reference to the Obama administration and the 'red line' concerning the use of chemical weapons in Syria mentioned in the previous chapter.

In Abrams' (2017) estimation, Trump's initial "national security team embodie[d] 'the Establishment' as much as John F. Kennedy's or Dwight Eisenhower's did" (p. 12). This establishment claim was based on Trump's nomination of former Generals James Mattis and John Kelly to head, respectively, the Departments of Defense and Homeland Security, former Exxon executive Rex Tillerson—a man with no prior government experience—as Secretary of State, then Representative Mike Pompeo as director of the CIA, and then General H.R. McMaster as National Security Advisor (ibid.). For Abrams, these "appointments suggest that, at least on foreign policy, Trump wants reliable people who will give him sober advice largely untinged by ideology" (ibid.).

Dana Allin and Steven Simon (2017) also described Tillerson and Mattis as holding "more traditional foreign policy views" in the context of US policy towards Israel and Palestine (p. 43). They also noted that Tillerson came to Trump's attention "with backing from three establishment Republicans, James Baker, Robert Gates, and Condoleezza Rice" (ibid.). However, Allin and Simon (2017) expressed concerns that Trump's alignment with "Israel's right wing" and "coldness toward the vision of a Palestinian state", among other issues, might cause him to deviate from a two-state solution (p. 37). In their words,

> the United States' strategic interests and moral values call for continued opposition to Israeli settlements in occupied territory, a continued insistence that the Palestinians pursue their cause through peaceful means, a continued commitment to a two-state solution, and continued attentiveness to Israel's strategic vulnerabilities. In other words, the most basic requirement is to do no harm, thus following in the tradition of past presidents. (ibid.)

In 2019, Simon—this time writing with Daniel Benjamin—described Trump's policies regarding Iran, specifically his "blanket hostility toward Iran", as representing "a departure from the norm of previous presidents"

(Benjamin and Simon 2019: 63). Philip Gordon, another Obama administration alum, wrote broadly in 2017 of Trump's early foreign policy approach. Gordon (2017) stated that so far Trump had "continued to challenge accepted norms, break with diplomatic traditions, and respond to perceived slights or provocations with insults or threats of his own" (p. 10). Seeing change and disruption at the heart of Trump's articulation of this approach, Gordon (2017) surmised that the "core of [Trump's] foreign policy message is that the United States will *no longer* allow itself to be taken advantage of by friends or foes abroad. After *decades* of 'losing' to other countries, [Trump says he will] put 'America first' and start winning again" (ibid., emphasis added).

Similar to Abrams, Daniel Drezner (2019) saw Obama and Trump as of a piece, specifically in that they both "have taken such pleasure in bashing the Washington establishment" (p. 14). Drezner (2019) also invoked structural checks and balances as a means to reproduce the concept that the US has—or has had—a consistent foreign policy approach. Drezner (2019) remarked that the "separation of powers within the U.S. government", mean "no one foreign policy camp could accrue too much influence", and has "ensured that U.S. foreign policy did not deviate too far from the status quo" (p. 13). However, Drezner (2019) argued that this consistent status quo, has masked "dysfunction that was afflicting the domestic checks on U.S. foreign policy" (p. 13). Drezner (2019) partly based this assertation on the claim that Americans do not think about foreign policy (an approach he claimed is "rational") (pp. 13–4). The other source of this dysfunction is the "marketplace of ideas" for foreign policy (Drezner 2019: 14).[1] For Drezner (2019), the "barriers to entry for harebrained foreign policy schemes have fallen away as Americans' trust in experts has eroded" (ibid.). Obviously, the history of US foreign policy is littered with a plethora of 'harebrained' schemes—e.g. any of the Mongoose operations in Cuba during the 1960s.

Drezner's reproduction of a status quo of consistent US foreign policy is reminiscent of the old trope of the US having an oscillating attitude to international involvement—interventionism giving way to retrenchment and back again (cf. Drezner 2019: 13). Like Drezner's invocation, this is

---

[1] In explaining why "hostility to foreign policy experts is not without cause", Drezner (2019) cited "interventions in Afghanistan, Iraq, and Libya" as "massive screwups" (p. 14). It is unclear how or why these interventions are attributable to 'experts', but not Presidents—particularly Libya in the case of Obama.

usually presented as emanating from a fickle public whose appetite for overseas involvement waxes and wanes, though less so in the post-WWII era. This is of course a vast oversimplification, which elides consistent international involvement pre- and post-WWII, and that homogenizes the views of a large, heterogeneous, and constantly changing population. Regardless, in this concept the throughline down the middle of these swings between intervention and retrenchment, is the 'status quo' of a 'consistent' approach, as in Drezner's argument.

This middle road—cf. Drezner (2019): "many of the guardrails that have kept the U.S. foreign policy *on track* have been worn down" (p. 10, emphasis added)—is essentially the national interest. However, as per the Wild Realist discourse, this national interest is not problematized as being a complex intersubjective narrative intersecting with multiple practices that are affected by constantly evolving domestic and international events and actors. Instead, this status quo approach is reflective of an essentialized US approach, an approach that simply always happened as a result of competing foreign policy views—with these views reduced to intervene/retrench. Or as Drezner (2019) puts it "Time and time again, U.S. foreign policy reverted to the mean" (p. 13). However, for Drezner (2019), Trump was more so a symptom of undefined "ills plaguing U.S. foreign policy" rather than the cause (p. 17). While Trump "made things much, much worse", he "also inherited a system stripped of the formal and informal checks on presidential power" (ibid.).

Such romanticization or simplification of the past—which we argue is a crucial aspect of Wild Realism's disciplining function—can be seen earlier in Drezner's article as well, when he questioned if "there is any viable grand strategy that can endure past an election cycle" (Drezner 2019: 11). Drezner (2019) stated that throughout the Cold War, "the 'loss of China', the rise of the Berlin Wall, the Vietnam War, the energy crisis, and the Iran hostage crisis, all overshadowed the persistently effective grand strategy of containment" (ibid.). There are multiple issues with such an assessment.

First, China was 'lost' in 1949, and though the 'Truman Doctrine' that underpinned containment was first communicated in 1947, it was not a clear articulation of containment (see: Acheson, March 24, 1947a; March 28, 1947b; Gati 1968: 138–9; also: Truman, March 12, 1947). Though elements of Kennan's containment were present in US foreign policy approaches 1947 through 1949, containment as a coherent, systematized strategy would not be implemented until 1950 in NSC-68 (Gaddis 2005: 87–8). Indeed, even by 1950 as the Korean war began, the Truman administration slow-pedalled the release of NSC-68's findings and logic to the public—including publicly linking North Korea and the USSR—as it feared a "war psychosis" might develop in a public already itching for mobilization (Casey 2005: 672, 668–70, *et passim*). Furthermore, the 'Nixon Doctrine' promoted by President Nixon beginning with his election in 1968 was a direct response to public concerns of overextension—exemplified by Vietnam (see, e.g., Nixon, Feb. 25, 1971). In many ways, the Nixon Doctrine was a rhetorical exercise in selling retrenchment packaged in internationalist tropes about world leadership to a US public perceived to be wearied by war. However, détente and triangular diplomacy, not to mention the US pulling out of Vietnam, were hardly in line with the containment strategy of the 50s or even early 60s.

Richard Haass also echoed themes of 'aberration' and 'tradition', while presenting overly simplistic historical accounts of US foreign policy. Towards the end of the Trump administration, Haass (2020) wrote that if the US had even "a partial restoration" to its pre-Trump foreign policy, then "Trump's foreign policy [would be] something of an aberration, in which case its impact would prove limited" (p. 34). However, if the Trump "brand of foreign policy persists for another four years, Trump will be seen as a truly consequential president" (ibid.). For Haass (2020), such a scenario would mean the "the model embraced by the United States from World War II until 2016 will prove to be the aberration—a relatively brief exception in a longer tradition of isolationism, protectionism, and nationalist unilateralism" (ibid.). Of course, 'isolationism' is not a foreign policy approach (and is ill-defined as a concept), protectionism of one sort or another never ceased, and regardless of the rhetoric of liberal internationalism, the US consistently practiced (nationalist) unilateralism throughout the postwar period (e.g., inter alia, Vietnam). Using a Wild Realist lens helps draw attention to the construction of a particular type of US postwar leadership, and the system it is situated within, as being threatened. It is not just the production of the threat that is performed here, but also the reproduction of a specific concept of what a US leader is/should be as well as a simplified historical narrative of US foreign policy intertwined with US identity.

By 2021, Haass had determined Trump was no aberration. Haass (2021) stated that though there were meaningful differences between Trump and Biden, they "obscure a deeper truth: there is far more continuity between the foreign policy" of Biden and Trump "than is typically recognized" (p. 85). In this article, Haass sees "elements of continuity" dating back to the Obama administration, which suggests "longer-term development—a paradigm shift in the United States' approach to the world. Beneath the apparent volatility, the outlines of a post-post-Cold War U.S. foreign policy are emerging" (ibid.). Haass' "old foreign policy paradigm" which preceded the new paradigm he sees, bears a resemblance to Drezner's vague description of 'containment' and 'grand strategy' mentioned earlier (Haass 2021: 86). Haass describes this paradigm as having been "founded on the recognition that U.S. national security depended on more than just looking out for the country's own narrowly defined concerns" (ibid.). Advancing and protecting US interests required the creating and sustaining of an "international system" which would "buttress U.S. security and prosperity over the long term" (ibid.). For Haass, this 'paradigm' was justified by the outcomes—regardless of "missteps (above all, the misguided attempt to reunify the Korean Peninsula by force and the war in Vietnam), the results largely validated these assumptions [of this foreign policy paradigm]" (ibid.).

Again, as with Drezner, Haass views disparate events and approaches as unified by (or through) a common strategic logic. Indeed, for Haass, there is a clear causative relationship between Cold War foreign policy/grand strategy (i.e. 'containment') and outcomes: "The United States avoided a great-power war with the Soviet Union but still ended the Cold War on immensely favourable terms; U.S. GDP has increased eightfold in real terms and more than 90-fold in nominal terms since the end of World War II" (Haass 2021: 86). It is interesting that the "misstep" of Vietnam—itself a direct outcome of an insistence on adhering to a 'strategy' of containment and fear of the 'domino theory' (itself predicated on the concept of monolithic communism, which had already been disproven) (see, e.g., Morgenthau 1967 [1965]: 41)—is folded into the containment/grand strategy narrative, rather than held up as a turning point in US foreign policy, a fork in the road towards retrenchment.

Michael Fuchs, in a 2019 article titled 'America Doesn't Need a Grand Strategy', claimed that the "gravitational pull for policymakers and experts to develop an overarching vision for America's role in the world [...] is strong and can be an important process that establishes policy priorities for the bureaucracy, sends signals to friends and foes, and helps evaluate assumptions and refine goals" (Fuchs 2019: 40). Fuchs (2019) also cautioned that looking for a strategy such as "the U.S. strategy of containment that was thought to have won the Cold War" has the potential to

54   D. MOBLEY AND J. GAZELEY

be a misguided and dangerous exercise, forcing simplifications of a complicated world and justifying counterproductive policies. Attempts at grand
strategy can become nationalistic rallying cries – like 'America First' or 'the
global war on terrorism' – that do far more harm than good. (ibid.)

However, this quote is indicative of the rest of Fuchs' article which
offers an oversimplified discussion of 'grand strategy'. It appears that
Fuchs equates 'grand strategy' with containment—"[t]he notion of US
grand strategy today revolves around American's Cold War foreign policy
of containment" (Fuchs 2019: 42). In doing so he conflates the articulation of foreign policy with broader domestic and political strategies. For
example, Fuchs (2019) laments that "some grand strategies are little more
than messaging exercises, providing a unifying justification for a broad
range of disparate policies" (p. 42), which appears to be an accurate definition of a key aspect of containment. There is also an oversimplification
when Fuchs (2019) states that twice since WWII the US "has adopted
grand strategies that garnered widespread domestic support and that
served as lodestars for U.S. policy—containment and the global war on
terrorism" (p. 43). While containment and the global war on terrorism are
broadly similar as overarching, master narratives—for defining threats and
US identity, as well as broadly characterizing or understanding conflicts—
they are not strategically similar in the context of foreign policy approaches.

Fuchs (2019) does point out that during the Cold War there was a long
list of "disastrous" aspects, including proxy wars, Vietnam, and
McCarthyism (p. 43). Likewise, he mentions that the global war on terrorism turned "the need to combat terrorism into an all-consuming global
struggle and attach[ed] it to the 'freedom agenda' that promised aggres-
sive support for imposing democracy" (ibid.). However, Fuchs seems to
overestimate the agency foreign policymakers—or Presidents—have in
shaping and controlling these 'strategies', and to underplay the agency of
foreign partners (see: Gazeley 2024). McCarthyism was as much a coopt-
ing of existing anticommunist discourses and disciplining narratives as it
was a foreign policy move—and it was not one led by a President. Indeed,
though the rhetorical touchstones of McCarthyism were foreign policy
related (i.e. that 'communists' and/or the USSR were attempting to sub-
vert US institutions and democracy from 'within'), it was very much a
divisive domestic strategy—and not one necessarily based on one person's
genuine concern for the safety of the state (Fried 1991). Fuchs (2019)
touched on this when he claimed that:

4   US FOREIGN POLICY COMMENTARY IN THE TRUMP ERA (2017–2021)   55

Obama attempted to reject the use of the global war on terrorism to justify policies harmful to the United States, but he couldn't completely escape it. […] Obama repeatedly attempted to place the threat of terrorism in context compared to much greater threats, but fears of terrorism continued to dominate the U.S. national security debate. Trump played on those fears by falsely linking refugees and immigrants to a terrorist threat. (p. 44)

While the global war on terrorism might not have been the best framework for contextualizing (or constructing) threats to the US, the choice of mise-en-scène—the rhetorical vocabulary—for explaining and understanding foreign policy was largely beyond Obama's control, as they often are for any president.[2] Not only does the public require some sort of narrative or existing logic to hold onto in order to understand threats and foreign policy (Hansen 2006: 25), but other political actors can leverage these narratives, as Trump did in this case. Fuchs (2019) describes "Trump's America First approach" as a "grand strategy of sorts", one he sees as capable of inflicting "significant damage" (p. 44).

In his conclusion, however, Fuchs still seems to either conflate broader strategies and foreign policies—or to misunderstand the inherently political nature of foreign policy and strategy. Fuchs (2019) claims that as "no single strategy will define the whole of the United States' purpose in the world", policymakers "should not submit to the false comforts of simplistic goals or ideological missions" (p. 45). Fuchs goes on, stating that policymakers "should embrace the complexity of U.S. interests in the world and dive headfirst into solving specific challenges like climate change and *not worry about whether there is a convincing narrative to explain it all* (ibid., emphasis added). Here Fuchs has essentially constructed a divide between nuanced, context-specific policy and more simplistic, ideological politics.

Anton (2019) reads Trump's nationalism as his foreign policy, going so far to label it (and his article) 'the Trump Doctrine'. Anton's conceptualizes Trump's foreign policy as an invitation for all states to embrace nationalism, which he interprets as a worthy crusade against the ills of globalization (which he compares to imperialism) (pp. 44–5). Anton supports his argument for this interpretation by conflating humans with states. In the first instance, Anton explicitly draws on Hobbes. After

---

[2] It also is not clear what specific instances Fuchs is referring to, as the Obama administration never substantially retreated from a 'terrorism' discourse.

claiming that "Thomas Hobbes is instructive", Anton (2019) describes anarchy:

> Not only is there no superseding authority, no world government, above the nation-state to enforce transnational morality; there is also no higher law for nations than the law of nature and no higher object than self-preservation and perpetuation. (p. 42)

Anton (2019) then goes on to claim that states "putting their own interests first is the way of the world, an inexpugnable part of human nature" (p. 42). Later, after an explanation of ancient animosities between Sparta and Athens, Anton asserts that differences between nations are due to various reasons, and that in this sense the differences between states are natural. In Anton's (2019) words:

> all these different factors, whether physical, geographic, or conventional in origin, are natural in the sense that they direct and inform a tendency that is inherent in human nature. (p. 44)

In Anton's approach we can observe a black-boxing of states. Anton (2019) claims that because of these innate human traits, "there will always be nations, and trying to suppress nationalist sentiment is like trying to suppress nature: It's very hard, and dangerous, to do" (p. 44). Along with conflating nations and states—or more to the point collapsing them into one concept—this approach effaces any domestic contestation within states (for example, between nations).

The flaw in Anton's arguments, which he himself gestures towards, is instructive. In Anton's (2019) words:

> Some Trump critics insist that "nationalism for all" is a bad principle because it encourages or excuses selfishness by U.S. adversaries. But those countries are going to act that way regardless. By declining to stand up for the United States, all Washington does is weaken itself and its friends at the expense of its adversaries, when it should be seeking to strengthen the power and independence of America and its allies instead. (p. 47)

The first two sentences reflect Anton's earlier claims about selfish states fighting for survival in an anarchic world, unrestrained by a world government. The third sentence, however, is an exhortation for the US to assert its power—presumably through a nationalist approach. However, if that is just what states do anyway, and if the nature of states and anarchy is universal and an innate feature of human/state life, then what is the benefit of a 'nationalism for all' foreign policy? Anton seems to be arguing that globalization and "supranational superbureaucracies on the scale of the EU" (p. 47) have the potential to restrain states (especially the US) from asserting this power.

States/nations are presented in Anton's argument as inherent, universal, and natural entities which are an expression of innate human characteristics. In this article, Anton does not substantively engage with concepts such as government, beyond a reference to "domestic or internal arrangements" (p. 42). However, Anton (2019) does seem supportive of democratic states—he notes that "Brexit and Trump" are a "normal response by beleaguered peoples who have been pushed too far" (p. 47). Anton does not extend this support to the EU, however. Anton (2019) conflates a general concept of globalization with the EU and then claims that in neither case has the process been "voluntary" for the "common folk" (p. 45). Anton also calls the EU a fraud and though he points out that members states had referendums on joining, believes this does not sound "like consent in the meaningful sense of the word" (ibid.). Anton goes on to state that had "European voters" been "forthrightly told" what the EU would do, "most would have instantly replied, 'No, thanks'" (ibid.). It is not clear what this assertion is based on, nor is there any mention of MEPs, or the European Parliament or Council.

While perhaps a bit of an extreme example, this article clearly outlines the differences between what is accepted as natural fact and what is perceived as arbitrarily constructed. Moreover, in the Anton example we can see how Hobbes—and various Hobbesian tropes—can be used to underpin a claim (along with invocations of thinkers such as Machiavelli (p. 45) and references to ancient Greek history) about state behaviour. Furthermore, Anton was Deputy Assistant to the President for Strategic Communications during the first Trump administration, and at time of writing, has been named as the next Director of Policy Planning at the State Department. As such, he is involved with foreign policymaking at the highest levels.

Conclusion

Overall, the expectation for Trump's first term foreign policy was disruption—for good or ill—to foreign policy norms. In many instances, particularly just before or early in the Trump administration, while Trump was expected to be a foreign policy novice and/or disrupter, there was hope and expectation that he would be reined in by an 'Establishment' cabinet. While the assumptions that Trump would be restrained by reasonable, experienced experts proved incorrect, so too did the essentially unchallenged view that Trump would have a coherent foreign policy, however disruptive.

Overall, the Foreign Policy Commentariat was unable to interpret Trump's foreign policy rhetoric as domestic, political discourse. While Trump's comments about, for example NATO, were generally recognized by the Commentariat as potentially dangerous, these comments did not translate into policy. Particularly in the early years of the Trump's first administration, but even towards the end, Trump's general lack of foreign policymaking was often interpreted as the expression of a specific non or lightly interventionist foreign policy (especially in light of Trump's comments about the wars in Iraq and Afghanistan). However, this alleged foreign policy was usually portrayed as a dangerous aberration from post-WWII norms—often using the old, vague bogeyman of 'isolationism'.

For all the damaging rhetoric from Trump and his first administration, in terms of policy and action, very little was done.[3] Trump did not have a coherent foreign policy approach. However, he did hesitate to use force and rarely took concrete action. Regardless, when viewed through the Wild Realist worldview, the Trump administration had to have a consistent, rational foreign policy and specific (non)actions which emanated from this policy. Trump was not criticized so much for inaction by the FPC– as this was often credited to a foreign policy/worldview based on retrenchment—but instead for not situating his foreign policy moves within an accepted framework and narrative of how foreign policy and international relations are conducted.

Essentially, Trump blundered his way through the events of his time in office with fewer perceived disasters than Obama (who admittedly was in

---

[3] Aside from a largely symbolic missile strike on Syria in response to the use of chemical weapons on April 6, 2017 (Lamothe et al. 2017), pulling out of the Iran nuclear deal in May 2018 (Landler 2018), and the airstrike killing of Iranian Quds Force commander Qasem Soleimani in Iraq in early 2020 (Salim et al. 2020).

office twice as long), a President with an active—and constantly articulated—foreign policy. However, for the Foreign Policy Commentariat both men failed to perform foreign policy expertise in accordance with the idealized presidential role. This ideal appears impossible to operationalize, resting as it does on the shallow Wild Realist framework which emphasizes rational agency and active decision-making in service of a quixotic conception of the national interest. Aside from the lack of a shared and operationalizable definition for this concept, the emphasis on rational decision-making which it pre-supposes underplays the essential randomness of foreign policy and the unpredictable events which shape it.

Indeed, in these assessments of the Trump administration there remained the assumption that the US was a rational, unitary actor. With this came the understanding of the US as a site of order and sovereignty exercising its power and responsibility in an anarchic world. Thus, US foreign policy and the national interest, among other concepts, were treated as ontologically given. And indeed, other states were conceptualized as objects without agency.

REFERENCES

Abrams E (2017) Trump the Traditionalist: A Surprisingly Standard Foreign Policy What Now. *Foreign Affairs* 96(4): 10–16.

Acheson, D (March 24, 1947a) *S. 938 A BILL TO PROVIDE FOR ASSISTANCE TO GREECE AND TURKEY.*

Acheson, D (March 28, 1947b) H.R. 2616 A BILL TO PROVIDE FOR ASSISTANCE TO GREECE AND TURKEY.

Allin DH and Simon SN (2017) Trump and the Holy Land: First, Do No Harm Trump Time. *Foreign Affairs* 96(2): [i]–45.

Anton M (2019) The Trump Doctrine: An insider explains the president's foreign policy. *Foreign Policy* (232). Foreign Policy: 40–48.

Benjamin D and Simon S (2019) America's Great Satan Trump's Middle East. *Foreign Affairs* 98(6): 56–66.

Casey S (2005) Selling NSC-68: The Truman Administration, Public Opinion, and the Politics of Mobilization, 1950–51. *Diplomatic History* 29(4). Oxford University Press: 655–690.

Drezner DW (2019) This Time Is Different: Why U.S. Foreign Policy Will Never Recover Searching for a Strategy. *Foreign Affairs* 98(3): 10–17.

Fried RM (1991) *Nightmare in Red: The McCarthy Era in Perspective.* New York: Oxford University Press, Oxford University Press USA - OSO, Oxford University Press, Incorporated.

Fuchs MH (2019) America Doesn't Need a Grand Strategy. *Foreign Policy* (234). Foreign Policy: 40–45.

Gaddis JL (2005) *Strategies of Containment a Critical Appraisal of American National Security Policy during the Cold War*. 2nd ed.. New York: Oxford University Press. Available at: http://ebookcentral.proquest.com/lib/ed/detail.action?docID=422884 (accessed 15 September 2020).

Gati C (1968) Another Grand Debate?: The Limitationist Critique of American Foreign Policy. *World Politics* 21(1): 133–151.

Gazeley J (2024) The Construction of Terrorist Threat in Mali: Agency and Narratives of Intervention, *International Studies Quarterly*, 68 (2), June, https://doi-org.ezproxy.ulb.ac.be/10.1093/isq/sqae056

Gordon P (2017) A Vision of Trump at War: How the President Could Stumble into Conflict Present at the Destruction. *Foreign Affairs* 96(3): 10–19.

Haass R (2020) Present at the Disruption: How Trump Unmade U.S. Foreign Policy The World Trump Made. *Foreign Affairs* 99(5): 24–34.

Haass R (2021) The Age of America First: Washington's Flawed New Foreign Policy Consensus Essays. *Foreign Affairs* 100(6): 85–98.

Hansen L (2006) *Security as Practice: Discourse Analysis and the Bosnian War*. New international relations. London: Routledge.

Lamothe D, Ryan M and Gibbons-Neff T (2017) Trump weighs actions in Syria attack. *The Washington Post*, 7 April. Washington, D.C., United States: WP Company LLC d/b/a The Washington Post.

Landler M (2018) Trump Abandons Iran Pact He Long Scorned: [Foreign Desk]. *New York Times, Late Edition (East Coast)*, 9 May. New York, N.Y., United States: New York Times Company.

Morgenthau HJ (1967) We Are Deluding Ourselves in VietNam. In: Raskin MG and Fall BB (eds) *The Viet-Nam Reader: Articles and Documents on American Foreign Policy and the Viet-Nam Crisis*. Revised edition. New York: Vintage Books.

Nixon R (1971) Second Annual Report to the Congress on United States Foreign Policy. Available at: https://www.presidency.ucsb.edu/documents/second-annual-report-the-congress-united-states-foreign-policy

Salim M, Ryan M, Sly L, et al. (2020) More Iran-backed attacks in Iraq likely, Esper says; Shiite militia boss killed. *The Washington Post*, 3 January. Washington, D.C., United States: WP Company LLC d/b/a The Washington Post.

Truman H (1947) Special Message to the Congress on Greece and Turkey: The Truman Doctrine. Available at: https://www.presidency.ucsb.edu/documents/special-message-the-congress-greece-and-turkey-the-truman-doctrine

CHAPTER 5

US Foreign Policy Commentary in the Biden Era (2021–2024)

Abstract This chapter examines the FPC's assessments of the Biden administration, by combining the gender analysis of the Obama chapter, the conflation of analytical concepts with ontological facts in the Trump chapter, and a postcolonial approach. In the Wild Realist discourse of the FPC, the problems of other states—especially non-western ones—are attributed to their place outside the US-led international system (itself a function of epistemological functions seen in gender/feminist theorizing). The threats faced by the US and western states are presented as universal threats to all states. The individual contexts of states are effaced and reduced to states either with or without agency, and as ordered or disordered.

Keywords Biden • Postcoloniality • Agency • Power • International system • Black box

To understand the mainstream of public facing foreign policy commentary during the Biden Era it is necessary to understand the political and intellectual landscape in which we find ourselves in the mid-2020s. At this point *Foreign Policy* (FP) magazine has moved away from its previous position as one of the twin pillars of the Foreign Policy Commentariat (FPC) and, presumably in search of sales, pivoted to become more of a general interest

---

© The Author(s), under exclusive license to Springer Nature   61
Switzerland AG 2025
D. Mobley, J. Gazeley, *Understanding Foreign Policy Commentary*,
https://doi.org/10.1007/978-3-031-95473-3_5

magazine. However, *Foreign Affairs* (FA) has stayed the course and became an increasingly central publication to understanding the mainstream of foreign policy commentary in the anglophone world. Indeed, as FP has stepped back FA has become more central to foreign policy commentary and public facing debate. Recent issues of this publication reflect a sense of profound crisis amongst the FPC. The overall tone of those writing in FA and FP across our period of study (2008–2024) has been consistently downbeat, with both Obama and Trump chastised for perceptions of declining US power. However, even against this downbeat long-term trend the negativity visible in FA during the Biden Presidency is notably more pronounced, reflecting greater existential angst amongst the FPC as a group.[1]

The cover of each magazine seeks to entice the potential purchaser, but also to communicate the essence of the content through striking visual language. The montage of recent FA covers below demonstrates both the pervasive sense of US foreign policy in crisis, and something of the worldview through which this crisis has been interpreted.[2] These covers suggest a focus on agency as a reflection of both power and the rationality to use it, as reflected in competition for the power to shape the international system itself. For example, the May issue of 2024 asks 'Can China Remake the World?' This cover is dark and moody with the Chinese flag rising sulphurously from a volcano, burning red and yellow like the eye of Sauron. The November 2022 issue and the January 2023 issue are focused on Xi and Putin, again focused on the world as shaped by these strongmen. The May 2023 issue is particularly striking, depicting a previously ordered black and white world falling apart on a red background, with red paint smeared across the sphere. The black, white and red as well as the angular black shapes and white sphere appear to be a visual reference to that most infamous Nazi symbol, which appears an odd choice for an issue supposedly about nonalignment.

A time of writing the most recent issue (September 2024) has the continental US 'Adrift' in the middle of the Atlantic ocean, alone, illuminated in a cold white on a grey-blue background. The US is here, despite the grim overall tone of this imagery, located in a commanding position in the centre of the cover, with South America, Europe and Africa gathered around it. Despite the 'self doubt' identified on the cover of January 2024,

---

[1] Though this may be reflective of the wider public mood as well.

[2] This crisis of confidence may be a much longer trend, extending beyond the period we examined.

it seems that the September issue still sees the US as the centre of the international system. The November 2023 issue depicts a shattered American flag, which combine with the title of the issue to suggest to the reader that the 'Sources of American Power' are perhaps not secure. The centennial issue of September 2022 speaks to an emerging, 'Age of Uncertainty', which perhaps gives some idea of the milieu within which the FPC are offering their commentary. The overall impression given by the progress of these covers across the Biden presidency suggests an increasing fatalism and disquiet amongst contributors to FA (Fig. 5.1).

Given this dire progression from the 'Divided World' proclaimed by the November issue of 2021 to the depiction of a US adrift in a world shaped by its enemies, it is no wonder that the July 2024 issue asks whether the US needs a new foreign policy. This question is posed beneath a twisted seal of the United States, with the proud eagle not only facing the wrong way but with its wings contorted, pointing unnatural directions. This most critical issue, which asks big questions about how to reform US foreign policy for the challenges of the present crisis, presents itself as a serious and policy relevant effort to 'fix' US foreign policy. This issue is primarily shaped by its contributors' concern with grand strategy (Rhodes 2024), strength (O'Brien 2024), credibility (Yarhi-Milo 2024), Great

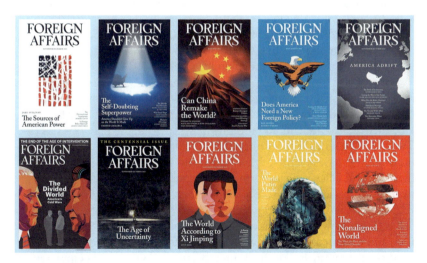

Fig. 5.1 Photo montage of selected FA covers from 2021–2024. (Cover photos from: Foreign Affairs Archives | Press Reader)

64   D. MOBLEY AND J. GAZELEY

Power competition (Westad 2024), hegemonic transition (Miller 2024) and the security dilemma (Glaser 2024). This issue is not solely realist but also includes articles which present an alternative conception of the international system, such as those on climate change (O'Sullivan and Bordoff 2024) counterterrorism (Cronin 2024), the Democratic Peace Theory (Doyle 2024), and even polling (Robbins et al. 2024). However, given that it also contains a reprint of a 1967 work by one of the fathers of IR Realism, Hans Morgenthau (2024), the editors are tipping their hand, revealing the significance that they place on works that are at the very least compatible with a realist conception of the international system.

Despite the sense of turmoil and crisis which this work has identified amongst the foreign policy commentary in FA and FP, there has also been significant continuity across the 2008–2024 period in US foreign policy commentary. This is partly a reflection of the linked Obama-Biden foreign policy community, which appears to place significant value on FA. For example, Biden's Secretary of State, Anthony Blinken, was previously an Obama adviser who publicly defended the Obama foreign policy in the pages of FA in 2012.[3] Jake Sullivan, the National Security Adviser, former Obama official and Hillary Clinton adviser, contributed frequently to FA on the topic of US foreign policy during the Trump years, and as a Biden official (Sullivan 2018, 2019, 2023; Campbell and Sullivan 2019). Articles with President Biden's name on them have appeared in FA in 2016 to tout the successes of the Obama presidency, in 2018 presumably to support a Presidential run and in 2020 to set out a foreign policy agenda immediately prior to that election (Biden and Carpenter 2018; Biden 2020).

Throughout his presidency, Barack Obama faced criticism from within the Foreign Policy Commentariat that he was not performing power in the right way, that he had in effect stripped the state of agency by being too reactive, too hesitant and too unwilling to make the big decisions (see Chap. 3). This was not a criticism restricted to his political opponents, although there was plenty of that (Rove and Gillespie 2012; Mead 2010). Even natural allies such as former democratic National Security Adviser and foreign policy luminary Zbigniew Brzezinski criticised Obama for his perceived weakness, imploring him both to "get his authority back" and "be a leader now" (Brzezinski 2013). In contrast, among the FPC both allies and opponents agreed on Trump's performance of strength, but differed on the rationality of the Trump presidency with critics emphasising

---

[3] See: Blinken (2012).

that this irrationality was the factor which undermined foreign policy agency in the 2017–2021 period (see Chap. 4). Agency, as demonstrated through the rational performance of power in support of the national interest, has also been a theme of recent appraisals of President Obama's (spiritual) successor, Joe Biden.

Unlike the Trump or Obama presidencies, the Biden presidency has been beset by perceived crises almost from the beginning. In the first FP issue of the Biden era, Graham Allison set low expectations for the administration, describing a difficult hand being played against the backdrop of declining American economic power; a "grave new world" in which, "grand ambitions will be constrained by diminished capabilities and produce diminished results" (Allison 2021). Carpenter was not so downbeat and was cheered to see Biden make:

> ...policy "built on a bedrock of science" a cornerstone of his campaign, over an incumbent president known for mistruths and conspiracy theories. In that sense, three crucial ideas that foreign policy should be made based on facts, logic, and reason rather than misinformation and emotion; that the United States cannot stand above or apart from its planetary neighbors; and that the perfect cannot be the enemy of the good—are not only alive and kicking but perhaps regaining lost ground. (Carpenter 2021: 49)

Hurlburt was cheered by Biden's lack of intellectual pretensions, arguing that his simple ways were an undervalued asset to US foreign policy:

> Perhaps that is because Biden comes to office at a moment of nostalgia for the great strategists of U.S. foreign policy. The media produces a seemingly endless stream of papers, op-eds, and tweets asking where the next Kissinger, George F. Kennan, or Zbigniew Brzezinski is and why the United States is failing to produce one. But rather than ask which Biden appointee will become the next Klemens von Metternich, we should instead ask whether we are framing the modern history of U.S. foreign policy correctly—and whether Biden's qualities, which at first seem atypical, actually help with a reset. (Hurlburt 2021: 36)

For Hurlburt, Biden's lack of membership to any particular school of foreign policy thinking offered the opportunity for positive change. However, Hurlburt sounded a note of caution arguing that he:

66 D. MOBLEY AND J. GAZELEY

[…] needs to transcend the foreign-policy paradigms that formed him. But he must also inspire a new set of categories by which Americans can judge him and around which a new coalition can assemble that outlasts the animosity to Trump that elected him. (Hurlburt 2021: 40)

There was, in this early phase, a sense of both the challenges and the opportunities presented by this historical moment. Of the need to rebuild after the Trump years, not only to restore, but to improve on what was there before (Tepperman and Zakaria 2021).

The 2021 withdrawal from Afghanistan shattered any sense of optimism among the FPC about the direction of US foreign policy under Biden. The chaotic scenes beamed around the world from Kabul airport by news networks drew significant and immediate criticism in the pages of FP and FA, with the Biden administration accused of lacking "resolve" (Al-Oraibi 2021: 7), "confused shortsightedness" (Pavlik 2021: 11) and abandonment of allies. In Labott's words:

When [Biden] and U.S. Secretary of State Antony Blinken talk of the enduring U.S. commitment to Afghanistan, they are primarily talking about finishing the evacuation. (Labott 2021: 9)

Despite some tepid support from Walt, who felt that this "admittedly chaotic ending probably could not have been avoided" (Walt 2022: 17), the fall of Kabul would become crystallised in FP and FA as Biden's first foreign policy catastrophe. This support over the Afghan withdrawal was also undercut by Walt's assessment, in the same article in FP, that:

…overall, there is little sign that the administration has a clear, convincing, and successful strategy in place. If one looks at the range of initiatives and responses they've pursued over the past year and a half, the record is unimpressive. (Walt 2022: 17)

There was also a sense that the Obama-Biden foreign policy community was showing its age, and had accumulated baggage, even though the Democrats were newly elected after an interregnum. The failure of the withdrawal from Afghanistan, echoed the Obama era withdrawal and then return to Iraq, and crystallised a foreign policy disaster which had been a long time coming. For example, Al-Oraibi explicitly links the Biden and Obama teams:

There were already suspicions in the Arab world about the Biden administration because of its officials' previous track records, such as Biden's position as a senator championing the partition of Iraq in 2006 and U.S. Secretary of State Antony Blinken playing a role in the Obama administration's refusal to intervene after the Assad regime used chemical weapons in 2013. A number of officials in the Biden administration—including Blinken, National Security Advisor Jake Sullivan, CIA Director William Burns, U.S. Agency for International Development Administrator Samantha Power, and Biden himself—were all at the forefront of making decisions during the Obama administration that contributed to mayhem in Syria, Libya, and Yemen. (Al-Oraibi 2021: 8)

As the Biden presidency reached an unexpectedly definitive end in 2024 many of the articles published in the run-up to the 2024 election assumed that he would remain the Democratic nominee. These writings reflected a profound sense of crisis and disillusion amongst the FPC. Given that 2024 was a high-stakes election year, and the incumbent had staked his reputation on his foreign policy chops, this bipartisan sense of crisis is somewhat surprising and reveals the underlying angst of the FPC. The FPC at this time mostly agreed on the challenges, China, Israel, Ukraine, Afghanistan, and frequently blurred them together to paint a picture of a singular failure to perform American power effectively. For example, O'Brien (former Trump National Security Adviser) points to Biden's perceived weakness in Afghanistan as an explanatory factor for the Russian invasion of Ukraine. He argues:

One can draw a direct line from the recklessness of the pullout in the summer of 2021 to the decision by Russian President Vladimir Putin to attack Ukraine six months later. (O'Brien 2024)

It is in this context of persistent handwringing over decline relative to China, and with three significant perceived foreign policy crises (Ukraine, Gaza, Afghanistan), that the apparent inability of the Foreign Policy Commentariat (as a group) to adjust their thinking is particularly striking. Unable, or unwilling, to move beyond an understanding of power as the organising principle for the international system, this group has also been unable, or unwilling, to adopt modes of thinking which are more suspicious of the concept of power itself. This is particularly clear in the 2024 FA cover article 'A Foreign Policy for the World as It Is', in which Ben Rhodes is clearly reaching for something new, using his article to call out a stultifying straitjacket of bad habits and groupthink, which he feels has led American foreign policy down a blind alley. However, whilst he critiques what he calls the "temptation to succumb to Washington's outdated instincts", (Rhodes 2024) his article nevertheless ends up reproducing that same consensus which he seems so disenchanted by. The lack of space to engage in terms of theory means that calls, even from close US allies, for a more fundamental rethink were frustrated, left without what the then German Chancellor called the "different mindset and different tools" (Scholz 2023: 28) necessary to dismantle what the then Shadow UK Foreign Secretary called the "assumptions the West made in the past which turned out to be wrong" (Lammy 2024: 128). Without the space to engage in retheorising such articles are left in the realm of tweaks, and fixes, doing better within the same system, when they appear to be calling for a more fundamental rethink of the system itself. In places Rhode's article even veers in a decidedly postcolonial direction, before ultimately pulling back:

> Too often, the United States has appeared unable or unwilling to see itself through the eyes of most of the world's population, particularly people in the global South who feel that the international order is not designed for their benefit. (Rhodes 2024)

This section gets halfway towards a plea for decentring the colonial perspective before snapping back, perhaps unintentionally, to a Kiplingesque implication that the ignorant or misinformed population of the Global South need to be educated on the benefits of "the international order". Here, Rhodes appears to suggest not merely that there are positive externalities from US dominance for those in the Global South but that the international structures through which this dominance is reflected and reproduced were <u>designed</u> for the benefit of people in the Global South.

Of course, Rhodes would hardly be alone in reframing colonial modes of wealth extraction as selfless and benign. As former Secretary of State Condoleezza Rice argued in a 2024 piece for FA:

> After World War II, the United States and its allies built an economic order that was no longer zero-sum. (Rice 2024)

This directly implies that the US replaced the pre-war European colonial order with one which enabled cooperation (within a zero-sum system cooperation is impossible, or at least inadvisable as there can be only a winner and a loser). Like Rhodes, Rice appears to believe that the post-war international system benefits everyone, through creating the potential for mutual advantage. However, Rice goes further arguing that the world cannot be trusted to function without US direction, without US maintenance of an international system, arguing (not entirely without merit) that in the past:

> Asian and European powers, left to their own devices, fell into catastrophic conflict. (Rice 2024)

Where Rhodes leaves this idea of Uncle Sam's burden implicit, Rice does not, despite her part in a neoconservative project which tried, disastrously, to put this worldview into practice at the barrel of a gun following the 9/11 attacks (cf. Schake's 'offshore balancing' below).

Mathews' (2024) pre-election evaluation of Biden's foreign policy record in FA was overall positive, and mostly supported his decisions to use, or not use, power. Ultimately this framing tells us little about the underlying foreign policy issues and instead more about the worldview of the commentator. A postcolonial approach to analysing Biden's foreign policy, even one premised on the same concept of power, might seek to interrogate what power actually means in this context. For example, is power the most useful way to view the withdrawal from Afghanistan? Whilst Mathews does not underplay this foreign policy failure, she does play a sleight of hand trick to move the point of failure far before Biden's presidency, and to reframe the decision to withdraw as a rational use of power, demonstrating agency, even though this decision was actually taken by the Trump administration and Biden was merely in-post for the operationalisation of this decision.

The question of power and agency is also essential to the way that Ukraine was used during the Biden administration as a way of keeping score within the pages of FP and FA. Annoying as it may be to Europeans to have their agency elided by a presentation of European support for Ukraine as a result solely of the resolve of the US President[4] (particularly galling given the brinksmanship on Capitol Hill with the Ukraine aid package, which was not seen in Brussels), it is far more damaging to Ukraine itself. The presentation of Ukraine as an object over which the

[4] This is also the presentation in Rhodes (2024).

two strong leaders, Biden and Putin, are tussling serves only to reconstruct Ukraine as a colonial object, which will be either incorporated into the Western or Russian system of satellite states. This focus on US agency, individualised through this conceptualisation of presidential strength, also serves to render Ukrainian agency invisible within the mainstream debate.

This denial of agency is also visible in Mathews' faint criticism of Biden, that he did not act to rein in Israeli abuses in Palestine (Mathews 2024). Besides missing the many ways in which Biden acted to shield the Israeli state from the consequences of these abuses internationally, and indeed facilitated the continuation of these abuses, this presentation also functions to deny the agency of the Israeli state. By writing from a presumed position of power, the explanation for adverse outcomes can only be the failure to deploy that power effectively. Writing in the same issue Richard Haass argued that:

> If success is defined as persuading Israel to adopt the course Washington wants,[5] then U.S. policy toward the country since October 7 must be judged a failure. (Haass 2024)

However, ultimately Haass and Mathews do not disagree that the failure to use power effectively was a failing of the Biden administration:

> ...the Biden administration has responded in a muted, ad hoc way, often with little to show for it. (Haass 2024)

Haass' article is premised, as is Mathews', not on disrupting or problematizing conceptions of power in foreign policy or in bilateral relationships. Instead, it remains firmly focused on assessing the effective deployment of power, which is objectified, reified and personalised. For Haass:

> One might expect that the United States' overwhelming power ensures compliance among allies, and often it does. But at least as often, power does not translate into influence. (Haass 2024)

---

[5] It is worth noting that Haass' definition of success echoes Dahl's (1957) textbook definition of power: "A has power over B to the extent that [A] can get B to do something that B would not otherwise do" (pp. 202–3).

However, complicating concepts of power, and locating agency in multiple places within a complex and dynamic relationship, would help to unpack the contextually determined limits of US power. A conceptual shift, which instead of viewing power as a reified *object* (which can be possessed by individuals or institutions), theorizes it as a *relationship* contextually and contingently constructed amongst the subjects in the relationship, opens up new ways of thinking about the foreign policy problems Mathews and Haass appear to want to engage with.

Walt, writing in Foreign Policy goes further than Haas or Mathews in critiquing the Biden administration's handling of the crisis in the Middle East. He argues that in practice the US "supports Israel no matter what it does" (Walt 2024: 8). Walt explains that:

> The United States' regional partners take its support for granted and frequently ignore its advice because they never have to worry that it might reach out to their rivals. (ibid.)

Walt, as could be expected from his prior work, is clear in his criticism of the Biden administration's handling of the Israel-Hamas war. He writes that the US under Biden was almost uniquely exposed to the charge of hypocrisy due to the mismatch between its moralizing and its actions:

> Nowhere has this problem been more apparent than in the Biden administration's tone-deaf and strategically incoherent response to the war in Gaza. Instead of condemning the crimes committed by both sides and using the full extent of U.S. leverage to end the fighting, the United States has provided the means for Israel to conduct a brutal campaign of vengeful destruction, defended it at the U.N. Security Council, and dismissed plausible charges of genocide despite the abundant evidence for them—all the while insisting how vital it is to preserve a rules-based order. It should surprise no one to learn that these events have severely damaged the U.S. image in the Middle East and in much of the global south or that China is benefiting from them. (Walt 2024: 9)

This echoes previous charges of hypocrisy levelled at the Biden administration over the Kabul fiasco:

> The juxtaposition may not be obvious from the United States, but it certainly is in the Arab world, where it is perceived as a glaring double standard. U.S. officials cannot claim a moral authority in the Arab world while standing

straightfaced and declaring the scenes around Kabul's airport were justified. (Al-Oraibi 2021: 8)

Walt also argues, from a realist position, that:

China has emerged as America's principal rival in part by mobilizing its latent power potential more effectively but also by limiting its overseas commitments and avoiding the self-inflicted wounds that successive U.S. administrations have suffered. (Walt 2024: 9)

Now, Walt is an avowed realist so his presentation of a realist worldview is neither surprising nor some sort of gotcha moment, as might be considered with self-described neoconservatives (Rice 2024), conservative internationalists (Schake 2024) or liberal internationalists (Haass 2024). We include him here to demonstrate the conceptual similitude between these very different figures associated with different political groupings. Their writings in FA communicate a shared belief in the centrality of power to explain international outcomes, in the rational and personalised exercise of this power by the presidency, thus transmuting power into agency. They are also all struck by the failure of this agency in the case of Israeli conduct in Gaza and their explanation is rooted in the failure of the presidential incumbent to use their power effectively.

VIEW FROM THE BELTWAY

The overall impression given by the writings of the FPC is that US foreign policy is the central concern of the world. This is not perhaps surprising given that all actors in a system are contextually situated and there is, famously, no such thing as a view from nowhere (Nagel 1989).[6] However, this myopic focus ultimately reproduces a colonial, metropole-periphery relationship of knowledge production with the world beyond the Beltway viewed as a stage upon which foreign policy can be enacted, rather than as a living world, peopled by actors worthy of understanding for their own sake. As with Rhodes and Rice above, the fundamental ability of the inhabitants of the world beyond the beltway to understand and advocate

---

[6] Indeed, this is also reflective our critical approach. In the words of Neal (2019): "The analyst does not have a God's eye view or a view from nowhere from which to construct objective and ahistorical definitions and concepts. Rather, the analyst's view is from a particular position within history, politics and theoretical debates" (p. 43).

5 US FOREIGN POLICY COMMENTARY IN THE BIDEN ERA (2021–2024) 73

for their own interests is not merely denied but actively overwritten as their lives and decisions are recast as background to internal Washington debates. This subalternisation is a related corollary of the denial of agency which manifests as a persistent, and jarring, US-centrism. O'Brien for example, exhorts FA's readers that with a strong leader who can perform strength on the world stage all will be put right:

> Another region where the Biden administration has demonstrated little strength and thus brought little peace is the Middle East... When U.S. allies see renewed American determination to contain the Islamist regime in Tehran, they will join with Washington and help bring peace to a region that is crucial to energy markets and global capital markets. (O'Brien 2024)

On the opposite political team, Rhodes seems aware that agency is not confined to Washington, and even includes the disclaimer that, for US foreign policy, "success is not preordained, since unreliable adversaries also have agency" (Rhodes 2024) But this still rings hollow, capping as it does an article which appears to attribute the foreign policy challenges faced by the Biden administration to his presidential predecessor:

> Trump's own presidency seeded much of the chaos that Biden has faced. Time and again, Trump pursued politically motivated shortcuts that made things worse. To end the war in Afghanistan, he cut a deal with the Taliban over the heads of the Afghan people, setting a timeline for withdrawal that was shorter than the one Biden eventually adopted. Trump pulled out of the Iran nuclear deal despite Iranian compliance, unshackling the country's nuclear program, escalating a proxy war across the Middle East, and sowing doubt across the world about whether the United States keeps its word. By moving the U.S. embassy in Israel from Tel Aviv to Jerusalem, recognizing the annexation of the Golan Heights, and pursuing the Abraham Accords, he cut the Palestinians out of Arab-Israeli normalization and emboldened Israel's far right, lighting a fuse that detonated in the current war. (Rhodes 2024)

This excises from view the fairly complex, long durée, historical processes which shape events across the world and presents them as the background for a palace dispute within the metropole over which geriatric Caesar should ascend the Eagle throne.[7] This is not to argue that US

---

[7] Unlike Rhodes, we now, at time of writing, know that it will not be Biden.

foreign policy under Trump has not had consequences for his successor, merely that it seems to overstate the case to lay the blame for the current Gaza war predominantly at the feet of Donald Trump.

This tendency to relate every major adverse foreign policy event to US domestic politics is not limited to Rhodes. For example, Mathews, who is a sympathetic commentator, praised Biden for his "masterful" foreign policy (Mathews 2024) and his ability to exert agency despite challenging material conditions:

> ...Biden's most important task was to restore trust abroad. He had campaigned on the slogan "America is back" and promised that the country would once again "sit at the head of the table." Once in the White House, however, he seemed to appreciate that neither U.S. power nor, as he frequently put it, "the power of our example" were what they had been. (Mathews 2024)

Rather than an imposition by external events (the ultimate denial of agency), Mathews' assessment recasts the withdrawal from Afghanistan as a rational decision about the employment of power—the very definition of agency for the FPC. For Mathews, Biden "[…] ended the longest of the country's forever wars—a step none of his three predecessors had the courage to take" (Mathews 2024) O'Brien (a former Trump National Security Advisor) took the opposite view, and accused Biden of "catastrophic mismanagement of the withdrawal from Afghanistan" (O'Brien 2024) and claimed that, "Trump would never have allowed for such a chaotic and embarrassing retreat" (ibid.). The debate here is clearly framed in terms of power, with the powerful Biden taking the hard decisions, or the powerful Trump not permitting such chaos and embarrassment to befall the nation. Furthermore, the human catastrophe of the failure of ISAF in Afghanistan is engaged with solely in relation to Red on Blue US domestic politics, not on its own terms.

Interestingly, Biden's phrase 'the power of our example', whether deliberately or not, demonstrates continuity by harkening back to a speech given by Obama in 2010:

> American influence around the world is not a function of military force alone... We must use all elements of our power—including our diplomacy, our economic strength, and the power of America's example to secure our interests and stand by our allies. And we must project a vision of the future

that's based not just on our fears but also on our hopes—a vision that recognizes the real dangers that exist around the world but also the limitless possibilities of our time. (Obama quoted in Al-Oraibi 2021: 9)

Indeed, this trope goes back even further. As former President Clinton said in a speech endorsing Obama at the 2008 Democratic National Convention:

Most important, Barack Obama knows that America cannot be strong abroad unless we are strong at home. People the world over have always been more impressed by the power of our example than by the example of our power. (Clinton 2008)

CONCLUSION

In the FPC's assessments of the Biden administration we see again a particular US-centrism. This is perhaps to be expected from US commentators examining US foreign policy in US magazines. However, the Wild Realist worldview precludes engagement with positionality. Again, it is not unreasonable for articles advocating certain positions that are made in aid of advancing a US national interest to promote this interest (however subjective and constructed it may be). Regardless, the world is made of many states with their own complex internal dynamics which then influence external dynamics in myriad ways. By assuming states are black boxes responding to events filtered through a US-centric lens, these analyses interpret factors affecting other states in terms of how they relate to the US. Through conflating the US with a US-led international system (or just the 'world'), such interpretations reconfigure circumstances affecting other states as being part of universalized problems facing states.

These universalizing approaches are intertwined with constructions and applications of power. The discussions in these texts about the appropriate use of US power situate this power in relation to other states as objects. This discourse then does more than just describe US material power, it also reaffirms the US as a (the) site of power in an international system. We see an equation made between agency and power—the ability to articulate and assert a national interest is power. This dichotomy also maps onto a subject/object dynamic. The US as a site of agency contrasted against the powerless and oppressed, the US as an ordered centre vs a disordered world of states. These dynamics are then reflected back on the application of US leadership. Discussions about the US president and his appropriate use of power become questions of agency, power, and responsibility. This is compounded by further conflation between the President and the US, and its responsibility to assert US power and agency in defence of its own interests (which are further conflated with the interests of a US-led international system).

We observe in this discourse a 'colonizing epistemological strategy' as mentioned in Chap. 2. Though we do not assert that there is an intentional approach by these commentators to marginalize or silence the subjectivity of other states, this is the effect of this discourse, nonetheless. Broadly speaking, the concepts invoked by the FPC—national interest, international system, etc.—were constructed in specific contexts with particular histories. Using them, particularly as ontological facts, reproduces specific functions. While the conflation of the president/US/international system are partially a reflection of the thoughts and inclinations of the commentators, this is also a function of the Wild Realist discourse itself.

The blurring of the lines between the US (as a unitary, rational actor) and a (US-led) international system appears to be a result of the projection of supposed US interests onto other states. It is also a point of distinction with academic realisms. The needs and problems of other states—especially non-western ones—are transfigured into ills inherent to their place outside the US-led international system, i.e. as a result of their non-western nature. Indeed, this is reminiscent of the discussion in the Chap. 2 of earlier feminist theorizing (itself a function of submerged, durable epistemological functions). The threats faced by the US and western states are presented, by virtue of their alleged threat to the international system, as universal threats to all states. This coincides with a conceptualization of states as black-boxed like units. The individual historical, cultural, geographical, and political contexts of states are effaced and reduced to states either with or without agency, as ordered or disordered.

This reduction to dichotomous hierarchies is indicative of a monological—that is, one way—relation of power, between the agential subject of the US and the passive object of non-western states (cf. Guillaume 2002: 11). This is a familiar function in the security studies literature. The Wild Realism discourse functions, as do security discourses, as "centring tales" (Huysmans 1995: 55). The identity that is under threat is placed at the centre of the story—at the centre of attention and focus—which is also the point from which the world is viewed (recall the view from nowhere mentioned earlier in this chapter) (ibid.). This function also creates a periphery, the place outside the centre—in this case a world of 'other' non-US states—where threats, disorder, and irrationality loom (ibid.). Finally, this mechanism reaffirms the centre (the we, the us, the self, the US) as unquestionable (ibid.). If the centre is the spot from which we view the world and narrate the story, then we/the centre are unquestionably real and ontologically valid.

REFERENCES

Graham Allison, 'Grave New World', *Foreign Policy*, no. 239 (Winter 2021): 17.

Mina Al-Oraibi, 'America Isn't Exceptional Anymore', *Foreign Policy*, no. 242 (Fall 2021).

Joseph R. Biden Jr., 'Why America Must Lead Again: Rescuing U.S. Foreign Policy After Trump', *Foreign Affairs* 99, no. 2 (3 April 2020): 64–76.

Joseph R. Biden Jr., and Michael Carpenter, 'How to Stand Up to the Kremlin: Defending Democracy Against Its Enemies', *Foreign Affairs* 97, no. 1 (1 February 2018): 44–57.

Antony Blinken, 'Morning in Mesopotamia', *Foreign Affairs* 91, no. 4 (7 August 2012): 152–54.

Zbigniew Brzezinski, Get His Authority Back, Foreign Policy, January/February 2013, No. 198, 56.

Kurt M. Campbell and Jake Sullivan, 'Competition Without Catastrophe: How America Can Both Challenge and Coexist With China', *Foreign Affairs* 98, no. 5 (9 October 2019): 96–110.

Charli Carpenter, 'When Foreign Policy Went Wrong', *Foreign Policy*, no. 239 (Winter 2021).

Clinton, B. Prime-Time Speech at Democratic National Covention. August 27, 2008. https://www.npr.org/2008/08/27/94045962/transcript-bill-clintons-prime-time-speech

Audrey Kurth Cronin, 'How Hamas Ends: A Strategy for Letting the Group Defeat Itself', *Foreign Affairs* (New York, United Kingdom: Council on Foreign Relations NY, August 2024).

Dahl, R.A. (1957) 'The concept of power', *Behavioral Science*, 2(3), pp. 201–215.

Michael Doyle, 'Why They Don't Fight: The Surprising Endurance of the Democratic Peace', *Foreign Affairs* (New York, United Kingdom: Council on Foreign Relations NY, August 2024).

Charles L. Glaser, 'Fear Factor: How to Know When You're in a Security Dilemma', *Foreign Affairs* (New York, United Kingdom: Council on Foreign Relations NY, August 2024).

Guillaume X (2002) Reflexivity and Subjectivity: A Dialogical Perspective for and on International Relations Theory. *Forum Qualitative Sozialforschung/Forum: Qualitative Social Research* 3(3).

Richard Haass, 'The Trouble With Allies: America Needs a Playbook for Difficult Friends', *Foreign Affairs* (New York, United Kingdom: Council on Foreign Relations NY, October 2024).

Heather Hurlburt, 'Inside Joe Biden's Brain', *Foreign Policy*, no. 239 (Winter 2021).

Huysmans J (1995) Migrants as a security problem: dangers of 'securitizing' societal issues. In: Miles R and Thränhardt D (eds) *Migration and European Integration: The Dynamics of Inclusion and Exclusion*. London: Pinter.

Elise Labott, 'Now the U.S. Must Help the Afghans Left Behind', *Foreign Policy*, no. 242 (Fall 2021).

David Lammy, 'The Case for Progressive Realism: Why Britain Must Chart a New Global Course', *Foreign Affairs* (New York, United Kingdom: Council on Foreign Relations NY, June 2024).

Jessica T. Mathews, 'What Was the Biden Doctrine?: Leadership Without Hegemony', Foreign Affairs (New York, United Kingdom: Council on Foreign Relations NY, October 2024).

Walter Russell Mead, The Carter Syndrome, Foreign Policy, January/February 2010, No. 177, pp. 58–64, Slate Group, LLC, https://www.jstor.org/stable/20684976

Manjari Chatterjee Miller, 'The Most Dangerous Game: Do Power Transitions Always Lead to War?', *Foreign Affairs* (New York, United Kingdom: Council on Foreign Relations NY, August 2024).

Hans J. Morgenthau, 'To Intervene or Not to Intervene', *Foreign Affairs* (New York, United Kingdom: Council on Foreign Relations NY, August 2024).

Thomas Nagel, *The View From Nowhere*, New Ed edition (New York, NY: Oxford University Press, 1989

Neal AW (2019) *Security as Politics: Beyond the State of Exception*. Edinburgh scholarship online. Edinburgh: University Press.

O'Brien, R.C. (2024) 'The Return of Peace Through Strength: Making the Case for Trump's Foreign Policy', *Foreign Affairs*, 103(4), pp. 24–38.

Meghan L. O'Sullivan and Jason Bordoff, 'Green Peace: How the Fight Against Climate Change Can Overcome Geopolitical Discord', *Foreign Affairs* (New York, United Kingdom: Council on Foreign Relations NY, August 2024).

Mel Pavlik, 'The Left Needs More Than Anti-Interventionism', *Foreign Policy*, no. 242 (Fall 2021).

Ben Rhodes, 'A Foreign Policy for the World as It Is: Biden and the Search for a New American Strategy', *Foreign Affairs* (New York, United Kingdom: Council on Foreign Relations NY, August 2024).

5 US FOREIGN POLICY COMMENTARY IN THE BIDEN ERA (2021–2024)

Condoleezza Rice, 'The Perils of Isolationism: The World Still Needs America-and America Still Needs the World', *Foreign Affairs* (New York, United Kingdom: Council on Foreign Relations NY, October 2024).

Michael Robbins, Amaney A. Jamal, and Mark Tessler, 'America Is Losing the Arab World: And China Is Reaping the Benefits', *Foreign Affairs* (New York, United Kingdom: Council on Foreign Relations NY, August 2024).

Karl Rove and Ed Gillespie, Opening Gambit: How to Beat Obama Source: Foreign Policy, March / April 2012, No. 192 (March / April 2012), pp. 22–23 Slate Group, URL: https://www.jstor.org/stable/23237844

Kori Schake, 'The Case for Conservative Internationalism: How to Reverse the Inward Turn of Republican Foreign Policy', *Foreign Affairs* (New York, United Kingdom: Council on Foreign Relations NY, February 2024).

Olaf Scholz, 'The Global Zeitenwende: How to Avoid a New Cold War in a Multipolar Era', *Foreign Affairs* 102, no. 1 (1 February 2023).

Jake Sullivan, 'The World After Trump', *Foreign Affairs* 97, no. 2 (3 April 2018): 10–19.

Jake Sullivan, 'More, Less, or Different? Where U.S. Foreign Policy Should—and Shouldn't—Go From Here', *Foreign Affairs* 98, no. 1 (1 February 2019): 168–75.

Jake Sullivan, 'The Sources of American Power: A Foreign Policy for a Changed World', *Foreign Affairs* (New York, United Kingdom: Council on Foreign Relations NY, December 2023).

Jonathan Tepperman and Fareed Zakaria, 'America and the World: How to Build Back Better', *Foreign Policy*, no. 239 (Winter 2021): 4–14.

Stephen M. Walt, 'Biden Needs Architects, Not Mechanics', *Foreign Policy*, no. 246 (Fall 2022).

Stephen M. Walt, 'What the United States Can Learn From China', *Foreign Policy*, 2024.

Odd Arne Westad, 'Sleepwalking Toward War: Will America and China Heed the Warnings of Twentieth-Century Catastrophe?', *Foreign Affairs* (New York, United Kingdom: Council on Foreign Relations NY, August 2024).

Keren Yarhi-Milo, 'The Credibility Trap: Is Reputation Worth Fighting For?', *Foreign Affairs* (New York, United Kingdom: Council on Foreign Relations NY, August 2024).

CHAPTER 6

Conclusion

Abstract This chapter reiterates the findings of the empirical chapters and concludes that the Wild Realism discourse of the FPC reproduces certain forms of knowledge and relationships of power through ontologising concepts and refusing to engage with the constructedness and plurality of analytical approaches. When these concepts are assumed to be 'real', these assumptions end up reproducing the concepts as universal. This is rarely helpful in terms of understanding the complicated and contextually dependent practices of foreign policy.

Keywords Foreign policy analysis • Worldview • Performance of expertise • Public audiences

This research began with a question between two friends and colleagues about public perceptions of foreign policy. Perhaps, we wondered, these perceptions are informed by general audience foreign policy magazines such as *Foreign Affairs* (FA) and *Foreign Policy* (FP). Given that they are the most widely read and highest prestige specialist publications on the topic of foreign policy, we assumed they would target a general audience. They do not really serve the small community of IR scholars, who it must be admitted, show little enthusiasm on a community level for directly educating the public. Moreover, IR scholars tend to publish in peer-reviewed

© The Author(s), under exclusive license to Springer Nature   81
Switzerland AG 2025
D. Mobley, J. Gazeley, *Understanding Foreign Policy Commentary*,
https://doi.org/10.1007/978-3-031-95473-3_6

journals and books, rather than these magazines. This led us to the question which has guided our, still quite exploratory, research: How have these mainstream magazines (FP and FA) presented foreign policy to the public since the financial crisis (2008)? This question led us to analyse the mainstream discourse of the most high-profile articles in these two publications (judging by their presentation in the magazines themselves and by the status of their contributors).

We have determined that, perhaps unsurprisingly for an American publication, these articles were (1) primarily focused on US foreign policy and US perspectives of foreign crises. Perhaps more unexpectedly (2) these articles were often centred on presidential performance, casting judgement on the incumbent through commentary. Most interestingly, through our discourse analysis, (3) we detected a shared worldview. We argue that this was shaped by the editorial policies of these two magazines and propose that it results from the attempt to minimise or excise theory from these publications. (And that publication of articles in this style attracts further commentators who favour approaches to foreign policy assessment which embrace parsimonious, theoretically light analysis). We conceptualize this worldview as a discourse called Wild Realism.

This discourse is more than the sum of its parts but is not a homogeneous worldview shared by every commentator in FP and FA. We propose that because of the editorial policies of these magazines, along with the types of articles and commentators that are prioritised, many of the analyses overlap in terms of concepts. Specifically, the lack of theory means that concepts are not treated as analytical tools, but instead as facts. While at first blush this might seem like a hardnosed, objective, empirical approach to foreign policy analysis, it is anything but. Ontologising concepts and refusing to engage with the constructedness and plurality of analytical approaches does more than just limit analysis. We argue that this worldview, this discourse of Wild Realism, reproduces certain forms of knowledge and relationships of power. As these processes might not be apparent to many readers, and because the authors of these articles frequently come from the highest levels of US foreign policymaking, it is important that the functions of this discourse are visible.

* * *

What empirical elements characterized this worldview? Decline and the loss of presumed US hegemony has been a consistent theme across our period of study[1] demonstrating the centrality of power as a presumed organising principle.[2] This is often personalised. For example, rhetoric of US decline was persistent in both FP and FA under the Obama administration, and particularly clear in the run-up to the 2012 election in a way which is difficult to square with the international situation. The great catastrophes of the Obama era, the moment when anonymous staffers would tell journalists that '*things really started to go bad*', (Rothkopf 2014) had mostly not yet occurred.[3]

These assumptions carried over into assessments of the Trump administration's foreign policy approaches as well. Writing in early 2017, Schake warned that Trump's apparent willingness to reduce international commitments and move towards "*full-fledged offshore balancing*", represented an approach whose "*weakness*" would quickly become apparent (Schake 2017: 45).

Similarly, in 2020 Brands et al. made a similar point about the Trump administration's Iran policies specifically, and Middle East approaches more generally (Brands et al. 2020). In Trump's response to increased Iranian military activity in the Middle East, itself a result of the administration withdrawing from the JCPOA and empowering hardliners, Brands et al. observed weakness. In their words:

> Trump's response then exposed the glaring contradiction at the heart of his policy: A president who talked tough and used sanctions aggressively gave the unmistakable impression that he lacked any appetite for the dangerous confrontation that was sure to follow. (ibid., p. 55)

Brands et al. claimed that Trump declining to "*punish Iran militarily for any of its provocations in the Gulf*" was "*[c]ontrary to 40 years of U.S. policy*" (ibid.). This analysis is itself set in a broader framework of power and interests: if the US is not willing to use its power and defend the regional order, Iran will reset the "balance of power" in its favour (ibid., *et passim*).

---

[1] A theme which also predates our period of study as well. See for example, John Kenneth Galbraith's article in the inaugural issue of *Foreign Policy* (Galbraith 1970).

[2] See for example: Economy 2024; Ikenberry 2022; Rodrik and Walt 2022; Rhodes 2024; Dickinson 2009; Mathews 2024; Sullivan 2023: Haass 2008.

[3] It was not until the second term that Obama faced the consequences of the intervention in Libya becoming generally known, the Russian annexation of Crimea, the rise of the Islamic State, and the use by the al-Assad regime of chemical weapons in Syria.

The Biden era coverage in FA is more complex than the merely faint praise doled out in 2012 to Obama. As the 2024 election approached, the pages of FA became a battlefield over Biden's foreign policy legacy with stern critique even from such a sympathetic figure as Richard Haass, who wrote that the US had '*little to show*' for its policy toward Israel over the Gaza crisis (Haass 2024). This was to some extent mitigated by Mathews' evaluation of Biden's foreign policy as '*masterful*', although even under the surface of this evaluation, there were significant areas of criticism (see Chap. 5) (Mathews 2024). From Republican aligned commentators Biden received short shrift, slammed for his weakness. O'Brien even went so far as to argue that Biden's weakness was at the root of all American foreign policy difficulties, and that with the return of a strong leader, Trump, these would melt away (O'Brien 2024).

* * *

It is not enough to simply perform expertise *at* the public. We must explain how we know what we think we know, and the limitations of our conceptual tools as well as the results of their application to contemporary foreign policy problems. We hope that this short Pivot begins the process of unpacking what the performance of public facing foreign policy expertise entails. The presentation of knowledge is never value-free or devoid of power. This is not to say that the articles of FP and FA are partisan or in aid of some hidden agenda (though perhaps some are). Rather, the performance of expertise and the dissemination of knowledge also represent the reproduction of relations of power. This is often an unintentional and occluded process—or a series of interrelated processes—that reinforce certain ideas as fact and underpin authority. These functions are not necessarily wrong or malign. However, they do occur and occur continually. For example, allusions to state behaviour in a world without rules may seem commonsense—and can be a useful shorthand. However, these are ideas that come from somewhere and when we start tracing back the threads of knowledge to Hobbes (and many others) we follow a trail of subjective, simplified and situationally contingent ideas. Likewise, even a notion as seemingly benign as the 'international system' is not, in the end, that easy to classify. There is no referent—no concrete thing out there—to which such a label can be appended. Yes, we can define a state in terms of borders, its sovereign government, or citizenry. But in terms of foreign policy—what is it? Does the state itself have human traits? Can it act as one unit? Does a leader unilaterally dictate its foreign policies? What about domestic politics? How does a state know its history, character, and traditional foreign policy approaches when it might not have the capacity to know or when many people may 'know' contradictory things?

While this may seem like a trip down a postmodern rabbit hole of infinite regress, it is far from it. Foreign policy is complicated, and we need different concepts to help us understand its constituent parts, relationships, histories, and mechanisms. And these concepts can be very useful for helping us understand what might be going on in the world of foreign policy and politics. However, when we assume these things are 'real', rather than concepts formed through our theorizations of how all these things might work, we end up reproducing these theorizations as universal. This is rarely helpful, in terms of understanding the practice of foreign policy.

We offer this Pivot as a starting point, an initial reading of the understudied empirical context of foreign policy commentary. It is not intended as a final word, but as an opening chapter to larger research project and an invitation for others to follow.

REFERENCES

Brands H, Cook SA and Pollack KM (2020) Why America Shouldn't Abandon the Middle East. *Foreign Policy* (236). Foreign Policy: 50–57.

Elizabeth Dickinson, 'New Order', *Foreign Policy*, no. 175 (11 December 2009): 29–29.

Elizabeth Economy, 'China's Alternative Order: And What America Should Learn From It', *Foreign Affairs* (New York, United Kingdom: Council on Foreign Relations NY, June 2024).

John Kenneth Galbraith, "Opinion: The Plain Lessons of a Bad Decade." *Foreign Policy*, no. 1, 1970, pp. 31–45.

Richard N. Haass, 'The Age of Nonpolarity', *Foreign Affairs*, 3 May 2008, https://www.foreignaffairs.com/articles/united-states/2008-05-03/age-nonpolarity

Richard Haass, 'The Trouble With Allies: America Needs a Playbook for Difficult Friends', *Foreign Affairs* (New York, United Kingdom: Council on Foreign Relations NY, October 2024).

G. John Ikenberry, 'Why American Power Endures: The U.S.-Led Order Isn't in Decline', *Foreign Affairs* 101, no. 6 (11 December 2022): 56–73.

Jessica T. Mathews, 'What Was the Biden Doctrine?: Leadership Without Hegemony', *Foreign Affairs* (New York, United Kingdom: Council on Foreign Relations NY, October 2024).

Robert C. O'Brien, 'The Return of Peace Through Strength: Making the Case for Trump's Foreign Policy', *Foreign Affairs* (New York, United Kingdom: Council on Foreign Relations NY, August 2024).

Ben Rhodes, 'A Foreign Policy for the World as It Is: Biden and the Search for a New American Strategy', *Foreign Affairs* (New York, United Kingdom: Council on Foreign Relations NY, August 2024).

Dani Rodrik and Stephen M. Walt, 'How to Build a Better Order', *Foreign Affairs* 101, no. 5 (9 October 2022): 142–55.

Rothkopf, 2014, June 4, 2014 Obama's 'Don't Do Stupid Shit' Foreign Policy—Foreign Policy.

Schake K (2017) Will Washington Abandon the Order: The False Logic of Retreat Out of Order. Foreign Affairs 96(1): 41–47.

Jake Sullivan, 'The Sources of American Power: A Foreign Policy for a Changed World', *Foreign Affairs* (New York, United Kingdom: Council on Foreign Relations NY, December 2023).

POSTSCRIPT

We submitted this manuscript in early January 2025, amidst an atmosphere of uncertainly about the incoming Trump administration's foreign policy. Of course, this book's analysis ends with the Biden administration. This was always our intention, and we still believe—even more so now—that this timeframe captures an important period in US foreign policy commentary. However, we felt it was important to note the dramatically changed, and changing, context.

So far there has been a significant shift away from the postwar norms of US foreign policymaking. Talk of guardrails, middle roads, and reverting to the mean now seems to describe a different age. While it might be premature to claim the second Trump administration represents the end of an era of foreign policymaking, it is difficult to imagine a rapid return to the foreign policies of the Obama or even Biden administrations.

As such, the foreign policy commentary analysed in this volume may document the ebbing of a foreign policy consensus. Whether it is fading into dormancy or history, remains to be seen.

St Andrews and Brussels, April 2025.

© The Author(s), under exclusive license to Springer Nature
Switzerland AG 2025
D. Mobley, J. Gazeley, *Understanding Foreign Policy Commentary*,
https://doi.org/10.1007/978-3-031-95473-3

Index[1]

A
Afghanistan, 50n1, 58, 66, 67, 69, 73, 74
Agency, 43, 54, 59, 62, 64, 69–76
Anarchic/anarchy, 32, 35

B
Black-boxed/black boxes/black-boxing, 75
Brzezinski, 33, 64
Butler, Judith, 18

C
Containment, 40, 51, 53, 54
Crisis, 51, 62–64, 62n2, 67, 71, 82, 84

D
Decisive, 33, 35
Discourse analysis, 13
"Don't do stupid shit," 39

E
Epistemology, 20

F
Feminism, 18
Foreign Policy Commentariat (FPC), 2, 4, 8, 14–17, 19, 33, 35, 37, 42, 58, 59, 64, 67
Foreign policy commentary, 4
Foucault, Michel, 15

[1] Note: Page numbers followed by 'n' refer to notes.

© The Author(s), under exclusive license to Springer Nature Switzerland AG 2025
D. Mobley, J. Gazeley, *Understanding Foreign Policy Commentary*,
https://doi.org/10.1007/978-3-031-95473-3

90 INDEX

G
Gender, 17
Gendered language, 35

H
Hobbes, Thomas, 20–22, 20n7, 25,
    26, 55, 57, 84

I
Idealized, 33
Indecisive, 34
International system, 7, 22, 23, 26,
    32, 41, 48, 53, 62–64, 67, 69,
    75, 76, 84
Intersectional, 17
Intersectionality, 24
Iraq, 38, 50n1, 58, 58n3, 66, 67
Isolationism, ix, 52, 58

L
Leading from behind, 40
Libya, 37

M
Masculine, 35
Miller, Arthur, 37
Morgenthau, Hans, 53, 64

N
National interest, 33, 35, 42, 48, 51,
    59, 65, 75, 76
Norm, 48, 49

O
Ontological, 14, 19, 23, 25, 76

P
Performativity, 18, 21
Personification, 31
Positivist, 14, 16
Postcolonial, ix, 25, 26, 68, 69
Postcolonialist, 24
Postcoloniality, 17
Post-positivist, 16

R
Rational, 20–22, 26, 32, 33, 48,
    50, 58, 59, 65, 69, 72,
    74, 76
Rationality, 35
Realism, 14, 15, 17, 22, 64
Realist, 16, 16n2, 20n6, 23, 34,
    35, 64, 72
Retrenchment, 50, 52, 53, 58

S
Strategy, 8, 15, 24, 38, 51, 53–55,
    63, 66, 76
Strength, 35
Strong, 32
Syria, 39, 40, 42, 49, 58n3,
    67, 83n3

T
Theoretical concepts, 23
Tough-guy image, 37

U
Ukraine, 67, 69
Unitary, 20, 20n4, 22, 43n15,
    48, 59, 76
Universal, 16n2, 19, 20, 22, 24,
    57, 76, 85

W
Weakness, 31, 33
Wild Realism, 14, 15, 17, 21, 26, 51, 76, 82

Wild Realist, 14–16, 19, 23, 33–35, 41–43, 51, 52, 58, 59, 75, 76
Worldview, 23, 33, 41, 42, 58, 62, 69, 72, 75, 82

Printed in the United States
by Baker & Taylor Publisher Services